SHIH-CHING

THE CLASSIC

ANTHOLOGY

DEFINED BY

CONFUCIUS

EZRA

POUND

HARVARD
UNIVERSITY
PRESS
CAMBRIDGE, MASSACHUSETTS

Library of Congress
Catalog Card
Number 75-37373
ISBN 0-674-13397-8
Printed in the
United States
of America

CONTENTS

PART I FOLK SONGS (KUO FENG)

1 CHOU AND THE SOUTH	POEMS	1–11	CHOU NAN
2 SHAO AND THE SOUTH	POEMS	12–25	SHAO NAN
3 AIRS (WIND) OF PEI	POEMS	26–44	PEI FENG
4 YUNG WIND	POEMS	45–54	YUNG FENG
5 WEI WIND	POEMS	55–64	WEI FENG
6 WANG WIND	POEMS	65–74	WANG FENG
7 SONGS OF CHENG	POEMS	75–95	CHENG FENG
8 SONGS OF TS'I	POEMS	96–106	TS'I FENG
9 SONGS OF NGWEI	POEMS	107–113	NGWEI FENG
10 SONGS OF T'ANG	POEMS	114–125	T'ANG FENG
11 SONGS OF TS'IN	POEMS	126–135	TS'IN FENG
12 SONGS OF CH'EN	POEMS	136–145	CH'EN FENG
13 SONGS OF KUEI	POEMS	146–149	KUEI FENG
14 SONGS OF TS'AO	POEMS	150–153	TS'AO FENG
15 SONGS OF PIN	POEMS	154–160	PIN FENG

PART II ELEGANTIAE, OR SMALLER ODES (SIAO YA)

1 DEER SING	POEMS	161–169	LU MING
2 THE WHITE FLOWER DECAD	POEMS	170–174	PO HUA

PART III THE GREATER ODES (TA YA)

PART IV ODES OF THE TEMPLE AND ALTAR (SUNG)

KEY TO PRONUNCIATION

The romanization of Chinese words adopted in this book is that of Bernhard Karlgren, except that his final *ï* is altered to *y*.

K, t, p are sounded as in French; no harm is done if they are pronounced as English *g, d, b*. When they are aspirated (*k', t', p'*), they are to be sounded as English *k, t, p*.

Ch is pronounced more or less as the English *j* in *John; ch'*, as *ch* in *Churchill*.

Ts and *ts'* can be approximated by *ds* and *ts* in *coeds* and *hats*.

J is as in French, but it can be pronounced as the initial *r* in English, which actually is the sound heard in Mandarin pronunciation.

Vowels are pronounced in continental fashion; *a* is always pronounced as in German *Mann* and not as in English *man*. In diphthongs each vowel is distinctly heard: *chou* would sound *jo-u* (*u* as in German *unter*).

The final *y* (*ï* in Karlgren, *ih* and *ŭ* in usual romanization, and *eu* in French transcription) is pronounced by keeping the lips parted and teeth closed while trying to say *e* as *shekel* or *jerk*. It occurs only in *chy, ch'y, tsy, ts'y, jy, sy,* and *shy*.

As for tonic pitches, since they are not marked they should be completely ignored.

In a few instances Mr. Pound has made arbitrary changes for the sake of prosody or clarity: *Wăn* for *Wen* (Ode 11) to make it rhyme with *clan; Ngwei* (title of Part I, Book 9) to distinguish it from *Wei* (Part I, Book 5); *Ghing* (Odes 178 and 238), *Mann* (178 and 256), and *Hsin* (236) to avoid confusion with English *king, man, sin*. The reader will also find that the demands of meter and rhyme occasionally make necessary a departure from the rules of pronunciation set forth here.

INTRODUCTION

by Achilles Fang

Aroused by the Odes;
Established by the Rites;
Brought into perfect focus by Music.

— K'ung-fu-tsy

A clever young man once asked Po-yü, Confucius' son, if his father had ever favored him with anything he did not impart to his disciples. Po-yü answered:

"No, he was standing alone one day as I was going by the court-yard, he said: 'Studied the Odes?' *

"I replied: 'No.'

"'Not study the Odes, won't be able to use words.' I went out and studied the Odes.

"Another day he was again standing alone, I went by the court. Said: 'Studied the Rites?'

"Replied: 'No.'

"'If you don't study the Rites you won't be established.' I went out and studied the Rites."

On still another occasion Confucius told his son, when Po-yü presumably had made some progress with the Odes: "A man who hasn't worked on the Chou-nan [Odes 1–11] and Shao-nan [Odes 12–25] is like one who stands with his face to a wall." With his disciples, some of whom must have been rather recalcitrant, Confucius remonstrated in these words: "Why don't you study the Odes? The Odes will arouse you, give you food for thought, teach you how to make friends, show you the way of resentment, bring you near to being useful to your parents and sovereign, and help you remember the names of many birds, animals, plants and trees."

What exactly, then, was the role Confucius played with regard to the Book of Odes which he prized more than any other? It used to be thought that he selected the 305 pieces from a corpus of some 3000 songs gathered over the centuries — a theory now generally rejected. In all probability

---

* The *Classic Anthology* (*Shy-king*, or *Shih-ching*) is commonly referred to as the Odes or the Book of Odes. For the sayings of Confucius (K'ung-fu-tsy) quoted here, see Ezra Pound's translation of the *Analects* published in the *Hudson Review*, III (1950).

the anthology existed more or less in the present form even before Confucius' time.

If Confucius was not the editor of the text of the Odes, he must have been their musical editor. Toward the end of his life, he claimed that after returning to his home in Lu from his final visit to Wei in 484 B.C., "the music was put in order, the *Ya* [Odes 161–265] and *Sung* [Odes 266–305] were each put in its proper place." It is possible that Confucius did set some of the Odes to music; but his admission that "when Music Master Chy began the ensemble finale of the fish-hawk song [Ode 1], came wave over wave an ear-full and how!" indicates that his actual role was to put an already existing body of musical notation into order, perhaps retouching it here and there. At any rate Sy-ma Ts'ien (145–86 B.C.) writes that Confucius sang the 305 Odes to his lute and made them harmonize with the modes of *shao, wu, ya,* and *sung.* (*Shao* and *wu* are believed to be the music of the legendary Emperor Shun and King Wu of the twelfth century B.C. "The *shao* are completely beautiful and wholly good, the *wu* are completely beautiful but not wholly good," says Confucius.)

The Master must have worked hard on the music of the Odes all his life. Whether at home or on the road, his lute was always with him; "barring cogent reasons, a scholar is never without his lute," says the *Li-ki,* or Book of Rites. Once he and his disciples were wedged in by two hostile armies for a whole week, during which time they did not taste a

morsel of food; yet Confucius went on plucking the lute (*k'in*) * and singing the Odes.

As to how the Odes were sung by Confucius and his contemporaries, only a wide solution, as Sir Thomas Browne would say, is possible. No music of the fifth century B.C. is preserved for us; we do not know even the kind of intervals used at that time. But, apparently believing that such puzzling questions are "not beyond all conjecture," a number of curious musicians have tried their hand in reconstructing the music of the Odes. The most important of such attempts is the notation of twelve

* This instrument is specifically mentioned in the Book of Chuang-tsy. Of the two kinds of lute, the *k'in* has seven strings and the *se* twenty-five. In the line "lute sound in lute sound is caught" (Ode 1) the first lute is *k'in* and the second *se*.

odes (nos. 1, 2, 3, 12, 13, 15, 161, 162, 163, 170, 171, 172) written down in the eighth century. Two versions of Ode 1 are printed here, one based on the original notation and the second on the revision proposed by K'iu Chy-lu in the nineteenth century.

For the reader who wishes to try the music, a syllable-for-syllable transcription of the ode as pronounced in North China ("a maunderin tongue in a pounderin jowl" — *Finnegans Wake*) is given here:

Kuan	kuan	tsü	kiu	tsai	ho	chy	chou
Yao	tiao	shu	nü	kün	tsy	hao	k'iu
Ts'en	ts'y	hing	ts'ai	tso	yu	liu	chy
Yao	tiao	shu	nü	wu	mei	k'iu	chy
K'iu	chy	pu	te	wu	mei	sy	fu
Yu	tsai	yu	tsai	chan	chuan	fan	ts'e
Ts'en	ts'y	hing	ts'ai	tso	yu	mao	chy
Yao	tiao	shu	nü	chung	ku	lo	chy

Of course there is no guarantee that Confucius read the Odes in a pronunciation like this (we know that both consonants and vowels were much richer in his time) or that he sang them in a melody reconstructed more than a millennium afterward. But it cannot be too strongly insisted that the Odes were actually sung in Confucius' day. Poetry to the ancient Chinese seems to have been an art in which the art of words and music formed a single unit.* In fact, the term "odes" applied to the 305 poems in this volume is to be understood in its etymological sense of songs meant to be sung.

For the past twenty centuries Chinese students have intensely occupied themselves in the study of the Odes; in this respect they were true Confucians. In fact, they could not but familiarize themselves with a book which happened to be approved as a canonical text. It was perhaps unavoidable that the philological problems embedded in their *Classic Anthology* were not seriously discussed. Research into these problems has been made only during the past three centuries. There is no doubt that most of them were solved by Ts'ing Dynasty scholars, who were formidable philologists. But it was only in recent years that scholars like the late Wen I-to have succeeded, with the help of compara-

---

* A volume containing a sound key to the 305 Odes (transcription of each syllable of the poems), along with the Chinese text in seal script and the present English translation, will be published by the Harvard University Press. Ezra Pound, who has agreed to the publication of the present volume as a step toward this fuller presentation, does not believe that "there can be any real understanding of a good Chinese poem without knowledge both of the ideogram reaching the eye, and the metrical and melodic form reaching the ear or aural imagination."

tive mythology and ethnology, in clarifying points left untouched by mere philologists. Unfortunately, more spade-work is yet to be done before we can claim to understand the Odes satisfactorily. Thus all translators of the Odes must take courage in their hands; after all, translators are interpreters among other things.

A translator of the Odes suffers from another handicap: Chinese scholars do not have much to tell him about the poetry and poetics of the Odes. Although men like Yü P'ing-po and Chu Tsy-ts'ing have recently contributed much to our understanding of the Odes as poetry, the translator still must shift for himself; he must, as Rossetti says in the preface to his *Early Italian Poets*, "cut various knots, and make arbitrary decisions" on his own. Furthermore, "mais d'abord il faut être un poète."

The poet Pound's career as a translator of Chinese poetry was launched with the publication of *Cathay* (1915), with which volume he became, says T. S. Eliot, "the inventor of Chinese poetry for our time." (The first poem of that slim volume is actually Ode 167; the appreciable difference between the present version and the "Song of the Bowmen of Shu" is understandable because in the earlier version Pound was at the mercy of Ernest Fenollosa's notes.)

As for Pound as Confucian, it is not known when he was converted; by the time he published his translation of *Ta Hio* (1928) he certainly was a Confucian to all intents and purposes. As the translator of the *Classic Anthology*, Pound now emerges as a Confucian poet. Instead of taking the present volume merely as another addition to the long list of Sinological translations, we have to "try with thoughts to comprehend the intention," as Hien-k'iu Meng was told by Mencius.

In this translation Pound, the Confucian, "the old hand as stylist still holding its cunning," is intent on fusing words and music. For this purpose the choice of the ballad meter is a happy one, as it not only makes the translation readable but accurately brings out the original rhythm of the Odes. For the Odes are essentially ballads; they were all sung, and some of them were probably dance-songs as well.

The *Classic Anthology* is divided into four parts: *Feng, Siao Ya, Ta Ya,* and *Sung.* The *Feng* or "Winds" (Part I, Odes 1–160) are folk songs of fifteen states in North China, of which four (Chou, Shao, Wang, Pin) were within the royal domain of the House of Chou. It has never been satisfactorily explained why songs from other states are not included. Conspicuously absent from the *Feng* section are the two states of Lu and Sung; it is hardly conceivable that no folk songs existed there. The absence of songs from Wu and Ch'u, however, has been explained by the fact that these two southern kingdoms were not within the orbit of China Proper — an explanation based on the political motivation that supposedly lies behind the *Feng*. It is said that there were Court Anthologists in the early days of the Chou Dynasty (1134–247) whose function was to collect songs through the length and breadth of the land for the sake of supplying the king with data for gauging the mores (*feng*) of his realm; in other words, the Odes served as straw votes. This Gallup-poll theory has some plausibility; since ancient Chinese were noted for their love of the arts and for their obsession with politics, to the extent of making a fine art of playing politics, it is not hard to believe that they managed to combine politics with poetry.

The difference between Parts II and III of the *Anthology* (together known as *Ya*) is far from obvious. The generally accepted view is that both are concerned with the political life of the day and that matters of lesser importance are in *Siao Ya* or "Elegantiae Minores" (Part II, Odes 161–234), while more serious matters went into *Ta Ya* or "Elegantiae Majores" (Part III, Odes 235–265). Be that as it may, some of the *Ta Ya* poems resemble those contained in Part IV, *Sung*.

Most of the *Sung* or "Lauds" (Odes 266–305) are hymns sung on formal occasions, such as offering sacrifices to the royal manes, or spirits, in ancestral temples. The inclusion of the Odes of Lu (297–300) and Shang (301–305) in this section needs some explanation. The Duchy of Lu was, of course, Confucius' home state; but this fact hardly justifies the exclusion of sacrificial hymns of other states from the *Sung* section or the omission of folk songs of Lu in the *Feng* section. Obviously something is amiss here. The same applies to the Shang poems, which have nothing to do with the defunct dynasty known as Shang or Yin. "Shang" here stands for the Duchy of Sung, which was ruled by the scions of the Shang Dynasty and from which an ancestor of Confucius, a royal prince, had migrated to the State of Lu. Possibly Confucius could be responsible for the inclusion of the four Lu poems and the five "Shang" poems in the *Sung* section instead of in the *Ta Ya* section of the *Anthology*.

Instead of trying to explain the three terms, *feng*, *ya*, and *sung*, by the content of the poems, some would accept them in a musical sense, taking the four parts of the *Anthology* as four modes with which to sing the poems. Ancient music being lost, such a theory must remain unproved.

Besides puzzling over the tripartite division of the *Anthology*, Chinese scholars since the second century B.C. have been cudgeling their brains in an effort to unravel the meanings of a triplet of terms applied to the nature of tropes involved in each poem and even in each stanza. *Fu* is narrative, *pi* metaphorical, and *hing* allusive. There is not only disagreement about the precise definition of these terms, but different writers have had different notions of applying them. These terms, however, cannot be lightly brushed off. Take Ode 6, for instance. What part is the peach tree supposed to play in a bridal song? Possibly there was some mythological connection between the peach tree and marriage; perhaps marriages were usually held at the time when peach trees were in flower, say in May. But the reader of that poem as a poem would not be too demanding if he insisted on knowing the poetic function of the *prunus persica, var. vulgaris* in an epithalamium. Literary scholarship should devote some effort to the perplexing problem of poetics; Chinese scholars have not yet made any systematic exploration of the world of imagery.

The Odes are said to give expression to *chy*. But the statement *shy yen chy* is essentially an etymological definition: the ideogram *shy* (Odes) is composed of *yen* (speech, to speak, to express) and *chy* (feeling, aim, wish, will). Even so, Chinese poetics has been dominated by this definition since the second century B.C., just as European poetics used to be dominated by the Aristotelian terms *mimesis* and *katharsis*. For the word *shy* soon came to mean, by extension, poetry par excellence.

Since the word *chy* is ambivalent, different writers could deduce different types of poetics from the definition. By emphasizing the emotive side of the word, Lu Ki in the third century wrote that *shy*, which he took as lyric poetry, should trace emotions daintily; this sounds very much like Pound's definition: "Poetry is a verbal statement of emotional values; a poem is an emotional value verbally stated." Usually, however, emphasis was laid on the volitional aspect of *chy*, with the result that the Odes (at least the *Feng* poems) were understood to be an expression of the wishes and desires of the often anonymous poets who wrote them. Supported by the Gallup-poll theory, this school of interpreters would stress the politico-ethical content of the Odes. Until the great neo-Confucian Chu Hi in the twelfth century discouraged this tendency, "orthodox" Confucians, who took the *Classic Anthology* as one of their canonical books, could not see poetry for politics. James Legge's translation of the definition, "Poetry is the expression of earnest thought," is based on the interpretation advanced by such "orthodox" Confucians.

Moreover, even before Confucianism received official sanction from the State, such interpretation seems to have been rampant. As a matter of fact, the Odes were sung or quoted on all possible occasions: in informal conversations, at convivial gatherings, on diplomatic missions. (And it was owing to this practice that the Odes survived the book-burning orgy of 213 B.C., for they were engraved in the memory of scholars.) Naturally it often happened that lines were lifted out of context. A certain Hien-k'iu Meng, for example, quoted two lines from the second stanza of Ode 205,

> Under the scattered sky all lands are fief
> all men to the sea's marge serve but one chief,

to prove that a king should enjoy homage from everyone in the realm, not excluding his own father. It was on this occasion that Mencius (372–289) counseled against literal and dismembered interpretation of the Odes: "Do not insist on their rhetoric so as to distort their language, nor insist on their language so as to distort their intention (*chy*), but try with your thoughts to comprehend that intention."

In thus insisting on the importance of context and sympathy, Mencius was merely following Confucius' precept. In the *Analects* Confucius says: "The anthology of 300 poems can be gathered into the one statement: Have no twisty thoughts." * This statement should be read in the light of another saying of his quoted as the epigraph of this introduction. Read in that context, Confucius must be understood as trying to integrate music with "rites" (*li*), just as he tried to integrate poetry with music; poetry, rites, and music were a single unit in Confucius' thinking. The word *li*, essentially a code of behavior, is generally rendered as "rites" when that behavior is directed toward the supernatural or the manes, and as "etiquette" when it concerns man's relation with his fellow men. Without going into a lengthy discussion of the term, we may recall Confucius' rhetorical question: "Are gems and silk all that is meant by rites (*li*)? are bells and drums all that is meant by music?" Perhaps the late Ku Hung-ming had an insight when he rendered *li* as "tact." It could, as well, be translated "character."

Confucius' statement at the beginning of this Introduction, then, may be paraphrased thus: A man wakes up with the study of the Odes, stands on his feet if he has tact (not only in the handling of men and gods, but in the reading of the Odes), and becomes perfect through musical pursuit. "Music," says the *Li-ki*, "is what unifies."

> And Kung said, "Without character you will
> be unable to play on that instrument
> Or to execute the music fit for the Odes."
> — Canto XIII

---

* *Sy wu sie*, which appears at the end of this volume. The three words seem to mean the same thing as "directio voluntatis" of Dante (*De vulgari eloquentia*, II, 2). The sentence occurs also in the final stanza of Ode 297, but Pound has apparently seen fit to leave it untranslated; he too insists on the importance of context.

PART

ONE

in fifteen books

FOLK SONGS
or "lessons of the states"
simple lyrics

I

"Hid! Hid!" the fish-hawk saith,
by isle in Ho the fish-hawk saith:
        "Dark and clear,
        Dark and clear,
So shall be the prince's fere."

Clear as the stream her modesty;
As neath dark boughs her secrecy,
        reed against reed
        tall on slight
as the stream moves left and right,
        dark and clear,
        dark and clear.
To seek and not find
as a dream in his mind,
        think how her robe should be,
        distantly, to toss and turn,
        to toss and turn.

High reed caught in *ts'ai* grass
        so deep her secrecy;
lute sound in lute sound is caught,
        touching, passing, left and right.
Bang the gong of her delight.

II

Shade o' the vine,
Deep o' the vale,
Thick of the leaf,
        the bright bird flies
singing, the orioles
gather on swamp tree boles.

Shade of the vine,
Deep o' the vale,
Dark o' the leaf
        here 'neath our toil
        to cut and boil

stem into cloth, thick or fine
No man shall wear out mine.

Tell my nurse to say I'll come,
        Here's the wash and here's the rince,
        Here's the cloth I've worn out since,
Father an' mother, I'm comin' home.

III

She:
        Curl-grass, curl-grass,
        to pick it, to pluck it
        to put in a bucket
        never a basket load
Here on Chou road, but a man in my mind!
        Put it down here by the road.

He:
        Pass, pass
        up over the pass,
a horse on a mountain road!
A winded horse on a high road,
give me a drink to lighten the load.
As the cup is gilt, love is spilt.
        Pain lasteth long.

Black horses, yellow with sweat,
are not come to the ridge-top yet.
        Drink deep of the rhino horn
But leave not love too long forlorn.

Tho' driver stumble and horses drop,
we come not yet to the stony top.
Let the foundered team keep on,
How should I leave my love alone!

IV

In the South be drooping trees,
long the bough, thick the vine,
Take thy delight,
my prince, in happy ease.

In the South be drooping boughs
the wild vine covers,
that hold delight, delight, good sir,
for eager lovers.

Close as the vine clamps the trees
so complete is happiness,
Good sir, delight delight in ease,
In the South be drooping trees.

V

Locusts a-wing, multiply.
Thick be thy
                    posterity.

Locusts a-wing with heavy sound;
strong as great rope may thy line
                            abound.

Wing'd locust, that seem to cease,
in great companies hibernate,
So may thy line last and be great
                    in hidden ease.

VI

καλὴ κἀγαθή

O omen tree, that art so frail and young,
so glossy fair to shine with flaming flower;
that goest to wed
and make fair house and bower;

O omen peach, that art so frail and young,
giving us promise of such solid fruit,
going to man and house
to be true root;

O peach-tree thou art fair
as leaf amid new boughs;
going to bride;
to build thy man his house.

To peg down the rabbit nets, observe his care;
good at this job, so also in warfare
                   to be his prince's wall.

Neat to peg down the rabbit nets
where the runs cross
and to be duke's man at arms
                   never at loss.

Deep in mid forest pegging the nets,
elegant in his art;
fit to be the duke's confidant,
                   His very belly and heart.

Pluck, pluck, pluck, the thick plantain;
pluck, pick, pluck, then pluck again.

Oh pick, pluck the thick plantain,
Here be seeds for sturdy men.

Pluck the leaf and fill the flap,
Skirts were made to hide the lap.

Tall trees there be in south countree
that give no shade to rest in
And by the Han there roam young maids
to whom there 's no suggestin'

that they should wade the Han by craft
or sail to Kiang's fount on a raft.

2

I've piled high her kindling wood
and cut down thorns in plenty;
to get the gal to go home with me.
I've fed the horse she lent me.

She will not wade the Han by craft
or sail to Kiang-fount on a raft.

3

I have piled high the kindling wood
and cut down sandal trees
to get this girl to take a man
and raise the colts at ease.

"One does not wade the Han by craft,
or reach the Kiang-fount on a raft."

X

By the levees of Ju
I cut boughs in the brake,
not seeing milord
to ease heart-ache.

I have seen him
by the levees of Ju, 'tis enough,
cutting the boughs, to know
he'll not cast me off.

Square fish with a ruddy tail,
though the king's house blaze, and though
thou blaze as that house, the faith
of thy forebears shall not fail.*

XI
MYTHICAL BEAST

Kylin's foot bruiseth no root,
                Ohé, Kylin.
In Kylin's path, no wrath,
                Ohé, Kylin.
Kylin's tooth no harm doth,
                Ohé, Kylin:
                Wăn's line
                and clan.

* Note: bream's tail supposed to turn red in danger.

12

Dove in jay's nest
to rest,
she brides
with an hundred cars.

Dove in jay's nest
to bide,
a bride
with an hundred cars.

Dove in jay's nest
at last
and the hundred cars
stand fast.

II

13

Pluck the quince
to serve a prince,
by isle, and pool.

Plucking quinces
in service of princes,
in vale, pluck again
and carry to fane.

In high wimple
bear to the temple
ere dawn light,
then home
for the night, leisurely, leisurely.

III

14

"Chkk! chkk!" hopper-grass,
nothing but grasshoppers hopping past;
tell me how a lady can
be gay if she sees no gentleman?

But when I've seen a man at rest,
standing still, met at his post,
my heart is no more tempest-toss'd.

2

I climb South Hill to pick the turtle-fern,
seeing no man
such climb 's heart-burn

but to see a good man at rest,
standing still, met at his post,
I no more think this trouble lost.

3

To climb South Hill picking the jagged fern
and see no man, who shall not pine and yearn?

But to see good man at rest
standing still there at his post
is the heart's design's utmost.

IV

Some reeds be found by river's brink
and some by catchit pool
that she doth pull and pluck
to bring by basket-full;

Be her baskets round or square
she doth then all this catch prepare
in pots and pans of earthen-ware;

Then neath the light-hole of the shrine
she sets the lot in neat array
that all the family manes come
bless proper bride in ordered home.

V

Don't chop that pear tree,
Don't spoil that shade;

Thaar 's where ole Marse Shao used to sit,
Lord, how I wish he was judgin' yet.

"Dew in the morning, dew in the evening,
        always too wet for a bridal day."

The sparrow has no horn to bore a hole?
Say you won't use your family pull!
            Not for the court and not for the bailiff,
            shall you make me a wife to pay with.

Toothless rat, nothing to gnaw with?
And a whole family to go to law with?
            Take me to court, see what will come.
            Never, never, never will you drag me home.

In fleecy coats with five white tassels,
affable snakes, the great duke's vassals glide
from his hall
to tuck their court rations inside.

In lambskin coats with five wider tassels,
affable snakes, the duke's vassals all
glide out to dinner
on leaving the hall.

With quadruple tassels or seams to their coats,
lambskin and all, with that elegant look,
noble vassals, affable snakes
glide out to consume what they get from the Duke.

Crash of thunder neath South Hill crest,
how could I help it, he would not rest,
            Say shall I see my good lord again?

Crash of thunder on South Mount side,
how could I help it, he would not bide,
            And shall I see my good lord again?

Crash of thunder under South Hill,
a fighting man maun have his will,
            Say shall I see my true lord again?

"Oh soldier, or captain,
Seven plums on the high bough,
plum time now,
seven left here, 'Ripe,' I cry.

Plums, three plums,
On the bough, 'Plum time!' I cry.

'No plums now,' I cry, I die.
On this bough
Be no plums now."

Three stars, five stars rise over the hill
We came at sunset, as was his will.
                    One luck is not for all.

In Orion's hour, Pleiads small
Came with coverlets to the high hall.
Sun's up now
Time to go.
          One luck is not for all.

Divided Kiang flows back to Kiang again:
abide us she could not,
abide us she would not.

Isles in the Kiang there be,
she so disliked our company,
Divided Kiang flows back to Kiang again.

As the T'o flows back to Kiang,
First she pouted, then she flouted,
          Then, at last, she sang.

Lies a dead deer on younder plain
whom white grass covers,
A melancholy maid in spring
                    is luck
                    for
                    lovers.

Where the scrub elm skirts the wood,
be it not in white mat bound,
as a jewel flawless found,
        dead as doe is maidenhood.

Hark!
Unhand my girdle-knot,
        stay, stay, stay
        or the dog
        may
        bark.

XIII
EPITHALAMIUM 24

Plum flowers so splendid be,
rolling, onrolling quietly,
a royal car with young royalty.

Flowers of plum abundantly,
Heiress of P'ing, heir of Ts'i,
to their wedding right royally.

Tight as strands in fisherman's line
may this pair in love combine,
heir and heiress loyally,
whereby P'ing is bound to Ts'i.

XIV
THE GAMEKEEPER
(model game conservation or it lacks point)* 25

Of five young wild pig he shoots but one,
        Green grow the rushes, oh!
White-Tiger is a true forester's son.

Of five boneen he shot but one.
        Green grow the rushes, oh!
White-Tiger is a true forester's son.

* Political allusion not to be ruled out.

SONGS OF THE THREE PARTS OF WEI
Pei, to the North
Yung, the Southern Section
Wei, to the East

BOOK 3. AIRS OF PEI

I   26

Pine boat a-shift
on drift of tide,
for flame in the ear, sleep riven,
driven; rift of the heart in dark
no wine will clear,
nor have I will to playe.

Mind that 's no mirror to gulp down all 's seen,
brothers I have, on whom I dare not lean,
angered to hear a fact, ready to scold.

My heart no turning-stone, mat to be rolled,
right being right, not whim nor matter of count,
true as a tree on mount.

Mob's hate, chance evils many, gone through,
aimed barbs not few;
at bite of the jest in heart
start up as to beat my breast.

O'ersoaring sun, moon malleable
alternately
lifting a-sky to wane;
sorrow about the heart like an unwashed shirt, I
clutch here at words,
having no force to fly.

II   27

Green robe, green robe, lined with yellow,
Who shall come to the end of sorrow?

Green silk coat and yellow skirt,
How forget all my heart-hurt?

Green the silk is, you who dyed it;
Antient measure, now divide it?

Nor fine nor coarse cloth keep the wind
from the melancholy mind;
Only antient wisdom is
solace to man's miseries.

III
LIMPIDITY

Swallows in flight
on veering wing,
she went to bridal so far over the waste,
my tears falling
like rain, as she passed from sight.

Head up, head down, throat straight the swallows fly
thru a haze
of tears, when she went to bridal
I stood at gaze.

I went with her toward the South;
up, down, left, right, the swallows cry.
I stood helplessly, as she passed from sight.

Chung Jen, deep of heart, taught
me in quietness the antient lordly thought:
sun's aid, in my littleness.

IV

Sun, neath thine antient roof, moon speaking antient speech,
Bright eyes, shall ye reach the earth, and find
a man who dwells not in antient right,
nor shall have calm, putting me from his sight!

Sun constant, and O moon, that art ever in phase,
shall ye pretend to move
over the earth
to find him who returns not my love,
nor shall have calm who makes no fair exchange!

28

29

Sun, neath thine antient roof, moon speaking antient speech,
shall ye range from the east
and find his like of evil reputation?
how should his course run smoothe,
forgetting love?

Sun constant, and O moon, that art ever in phase,
up from the east always; father and mother mine
that have of me no care,
shall ye not pine
that guard not my right!

V

THE MARQUISE CHUANG KIANG

against her husband 30

Cold parcheth the end wind, colder mockery,
Frigid the smile to my heart's misery.

Dust in the wind and sand; what should a promise be?
You promise and do not come, yet stand
in my heart constantly.

The wind has blown the sky
to one black solid cloud, all the day long
night long I sleep not
seeking to mutter this wrong.

Under black solid cloud,
thunder, thunder so loud I sleep not,
seeking to speak its thought.

VI 31

Bang, the drum. We jump and drill,
some folks are working on Ts'ao Wall still
or hauling farm loads in Ts'ao
but we're on the roads, south, on the roads

under Tsy Chung.
Sung and Ch'en come.
We've rolled 'em flat but
we'll never get home.

To stay together till death and end
for far, for near, hand, oath, accord:
Never alive
will we keep that word.

VII

Soft wind from South to find
what is in the thorn-tree's mind;
thorn-tree's mind, tender and fair,
our mother thorned down with care.

South wind on fagot
that was tree when
she thought of goodness,
yet made us not thoughtful men.

Smooth the cool spring of Tsün
flows to the lower soil,
seven sons had our mother
worn hard with toil;

Yellow bird's beauty
makes good in song,
seven sons
do her wrong.

VIII

Pheasant-cock flies on easy wing,
absent lord, to my sorrowing.

As the bright pheasant flies
wind lowers and lifts the tone;
sorrow: my lord gone out,
I am alone.

Look up to the sun and moon
in my thought the long pain,
the road is so long, how
shall he come again.

Ye hundred gentlemen, conscienceless
in your acts, say true:
He neither hates nor covets,
what wrong shall he do?

BOTTLE—GOURD

Bitter the gourd leaf, passed the high-water mark,
"Let the deep drench, o'er shallows lift a sark!"

At the over-flooded ford: "Won't wet an axle block!"
Hen pheasant cries, seeking her pheasant-cock.

Tranquil the wild goose's note
at sunrise, ere ice gins thaw,
noble takes mate
observing the antient law.

Boatman cocks thumb, some go,
I do not so,
Waiting till my man come.

THE EFFICIENT WIFE'S COMPLAINT

Wind o' the East dark with rain,
a man should not bring his olde wife pain
but should bide concordantly.
Gather *feng* gather *fei*,
man can eat and live thereby,
Now what fault is spoke against me
that I should not wedded die?

Slow road go I, mid-heart in pain,
You scarce came to my domain.
Who saith now the thistle scratches?
Soft as shepherd's-purse that matches
your new leman feasts with you
in full joy as brothers do.

King River 's muddied by the Wei
yet pools to clearness presently.
You feast your doxy now she 's new
and with me will naught to do.
So come not near my dam and weir,
let my fish-basket be,
In your hate what hold have I,
Indifferent all futurity!

Ready to raft the deep,
wade shallow or dive for gain —
sharing both had and lost —
and help the destitute
whate'er it cost

Not your heart's garden now,
an opponent,
you lower my market price
blocking my good intent.
I worked when we were poor and took no heed,
whom you, now rich, compare to poison weed.

I piled good store to last the winter through
so now you feast, and your new doxy 's new.
'Twas I who saved for winter and you who spent,
mine the real work, you now wax violent
forgetting all the past for good or best
when 'twas with me alone that you found rest.

XI
(KING CHARLES)   36

Why? why?

By the Lord Wei,
For the Lord Wei this misery
sleeping in dew.
Never pull through!

Worse, worse!
Say that we could
go home but for his noble blood.

Sleeping in mud,
why? why?

For Milord Wei.

XII   37

Mao Mount's vine-joints show their age,
Uncles and nobles, how many days?

Why delay here with no allies;
Why delay here in lack of supplies?

Fox furs worn thru, without transport,
Uncles and nobles, sorry sport!

We be the rump of Li with tattered tails,
a lost horde amid fears,
and your embroidered collars
cover your ears.

XIII

GUARDSMAN IN BALLET

38

Élite (or ee-light) ready on the dot
for court theatrical
even at mid-day, by the upper loge
in the Duke's court, and I am tall,
strong as a tiger, to whom horse-reins are silk.

A flute in left hand, in my right a fan;
red as if varnished when the duke sends wine,
                                    a man?

Hazel on hill, mallow in mead,
West Country men for prettiness, who guessed?
What ass would say: this beauty 's from the West?

XIV

BRIDE'S NOSTALGIA FOR HOME FOLKS

39

Ware spring water that flows to the K'i,
flowing thought is jeopardy.
Every day my thought 's in Wei,
where pretty cousins would talk to me
we would devise right pleasantly.

To Tsy for the night, and farewell cup at Ni;
When a girl marries she goes out
far from her parents and close male kin;
there's a feast and she
asks her aunts and sisters all in.

Now I would night by Kan and Yen.
"Grease the axle and fix the lynch-pin"
anything to get quickly to Wei
without roadside calamity.

"By Fei-Ts'üan's winding stream"
of Sü and Ts'ao is all my dream,
and all I can get is a p.m. drive
to keep my inner life alive.

XV

North gate, sorrow's edge,
purse kaput, nothing to pledge.

I'll say I'm broke
none knows how, heaven's stroke.

Government work piled up on me.

When I go back where I lived before,
my dear relatives slam the door.
This is the job put up on me,
Sky's "which and how"?
or say: destiny.

Government work piled up on me.

When I come in from being out
my home-folk don't want me about;
concrete fruit of heaven's tree
not to be changed by verbosity.

XVI

Cold wind, and rain
North snows again.
   Kindly who love me, take hands and go!
   Make haste,
    State 's waste!

Sougheth to North,
Sleeteth cold snow,
   Kindly who love me, take hands and go!

All red things foxes, each black a crow
(evils in omen) love me, and go
    State 's waste.
    Make haste
      and
      go.

THE APPOINTMENT MANQUÉ

Lady of azure thought, supple and tall,
I wait by nook, by angle in the wall,
love and see naught; shift foot and scratch my poll.

Lady of silken word, in clarity
gavest a reed whereon red flower flamed less
than thy delightfulness.

In mead she plucked the *molu* grass,
fair as streamlet did she pass.

"Reed, art to prize in thy beauty,
        but more that frail, who gave thee me."

XVIII
"Satire on the marriage
of Duke Süan"

New tower's sheen reflected full in Ho,
She sought a beau
with whom to curl at eve.

She sought a beau with whom to curl at eve
By tower, by Ho, by flow and got
His ruckling relative.

Goose to get in a fish-net set!
His ruckling relative.

XIX
"Rumours as to the death
of Süan's sons"

A boat floats over shadow, two boys were aboard.
There is a cloud over my thought
and of them no word.

The boat floats past the sky's edge, lank sail a-flap;
and a dark thought inside me: how had they hap?

45

Pine boat a-drift in Ho,
dark drifts the tufted hair.
Mated we were till death,
> Shall no one keep faith?
> Mother of Heaven,
> Shall no one keep faith!

Boat drifts to the shore,
Dark tufts float in the waste.
My bull till death he were,
> Shall no one be traist?
> Mother of Heaven,
> Shall no one be traist! *

II
(Three strophes with negligible variations)

46

The things they do and the things they say
> in the harem,
> in the harem,
There is no end to the things they say in the harem,
There is no shame in the things they say in the harem,
> So pull not the vine away.

III
CAESAR'S WIFE

47

Go with him for a life long
with high jewelled hair-do,
Stately as a hill,
suave as a mountain stream
> Show gown,
> Show gown,
> > and yet?

* She refuses to marry again

Cloak like a pheasant,
Hair like a storm cloud, jade in her ears,
High comb of ivory set
white as her forehead,
                    Diva,
                    Diva,
                              and yet?

Splendour at court high guests to entertain,
erudite silk or plain flax in the grain,
above it all the clear spread of her brows:
"Surely of dames this is the cynosure,
the pride of ladies and the land's allure!"
                              and yet?

IV

THE CONSTANT LOVER

To gather the "gold thread" south of Mei,
Who saith 'tis fantasy?

Mid the mulberry trees of Sang Chung
said: "In Shang Kung," Miss Kiang to me,

          "And then a week-end on the K'i."

To take in wheat crop, north of Mei,
Who saith 'tis fantasy?

Mid the mulberry trees of Sang Chung
said: "In Shang Kung," to me the first Miss Yi

          "And then a week-end on the K'i."

To get in mustard east of Mei,
Who saith 'tis fantasy?

Mid the mulberry trees of Sang Chung
said: "In Shang Kung," Miss Yung to me

          "And then a week-end on the K'i."

V

Quails and pies
show enmities,
but a man with *no* savoury quality
is my own brother apparently.

Pies and quails
tear each other's entrails
and there's a fair lady would do no less:
Let me present our Marchioness.

VI

TING

the star of quiet course, marking the time
to end field work

The star of quiet being in mid-sky,
he reared up Bramble hall;
took sun to measure the wall;
planted abundantly
chestnut and hazel tree;
tung tree and varnish roots
whence wood to make our lutes.

He clomb the waste-land there to spy
how Ch'u and T'ang lands lie;
measured to fit the shadow's fall
mountain site for his capital,
orchard space lying under it all.
Then he took augury
of how things by right should be;
learned from the shell what was eventually,
that is, the event in its probity.

On timely rainfall in the starlit gloom,
would call his groom to hitch
ere day was come,
"To orchard and sown!" he'ld say,
so straight a man, the course
of heart so deep
that gave him three thousand tall horse.

VII

NO TRUST IN RAINBOWS

51

Rainbow duplex in East
no one dares trust in,
girl going out must
leave afar her kin.

...UITY AND SANS POISE
"Dentes habet."
                                    Catullus   52

. rat too has a skin (to tan)
A rat has a skin at least
But a man who is a mere beast
might as well die,
his death being end of no decency.

A rat also has teeth
but this fellow, for all his size, is beneath
the rat's level,
why delay his demise?

The rat also has feet
but a man without courtesy need not wait
to clutter hell's gate.

Why should a man of no moral worth
clutter the earth?
This fellow's beneath the rat's modus,
why delay his exodus?

A man without courtesy
might quite as well cease to be.

                    IX   53

Ox tails flap from the pikes
outside the market dykes
at Tsün;

Yak tails with plain silk bands,
The quadriga stands to wait an honoured guest
whose fame deserves our best.

Let falcon banners fly by Tsün
and silken panoply
float beyond moat in capital.
Five horses wait;
is not this fitting state?

The plumed flags fold and fall
above Tsün's wall
with white silk bands.
Six horsemen in full state
stand to felicitate
a guest
whose fame deserves our best.

X
**Baroness Mu impeded in her wish
to help famine victims in Wei**

I wanted to harness and go
share woe in Wei,
I would have made Ts'ao my first halt,
It was never my fault
that a deputy went to my brother
across grass and water,
could he carry my grief?

Without your visa I could not go,
I cannot honour your act
nor retract.
My sympathy was real, your's the offence
if I cannot carry my condolence.
Wrongly you wrought.
I cannot stifle my thought.

(Without your visa, does honour requite it so?)

Nor was my thought wrong in this
you would not approve.
I cannot take home my condolence,
If thus wrongly you wrought,
I cannot stifle my thought.

I climb the cornered hill seeking heart's ease,
If sorrow be real, let heart with sorrow's load
go its sole road.

The Hü crowd's vulgar cry
sounds out presumptuously.
I wanted to go to the plains
where the thick grain is.
I would have asked aid of great states,
their kings and great potentates;
some would deny, some do their most,
but I would have had no blame.

All your hundred plans come to naught,
none matched my thought.

BOOK 5. WEI WIND

I

πολύμητις

**The bamboos grow well
under good rule**

55

Dry in the sun by corner of K'i
green bamboo, bole over bole:
Such subtle prince is ours
to grind and file his powers
as jade is ground by wheel;
he careth his people's weal,
stern in attent,
steady as sun's turn bent
on his folk's betterment
                    nor will he fail.

Look ye here on the coves of the K'i:
green bamboo glitteringly!
Of as fine grain our prince appears
as the jasper plugs in his ears
ground bright as the stars in his cap of state;
his acumen in debate

splendid, steadfast in judgement-hall
he cannot fail us
                   nor fall.

In coves of K'i,
bamboo in leaf abundantly.
As metal tried is fine
or as sceptre of jade is clean;
stern in his amplitude,
magnanimous to enforce true laws, or lean
over chariot rail in humour
as he were a tiger
                   with velvet paws.

II

Made his hut in the vale, a tall man stretched out
sleeps, wakes and says: no room for doubt.

Lean-to on torrent's brink, laughter in idleness,
sleeps, wakes and sings; I will move less.

In a hut on a butte, himself his pivot, sleeps,
wakes, sleeps again,
swearing he will not communicate
with other men.

III
EPITHALAMIUM
"Sidney's sister"

Tall girl with a profile,
broidery neath a simple dress,
brought from Ts'i her loveliness
to Wei's marquisat.

Younger sister of Tung-Kung
("Palace of the East," crown-prince)
One sister of hers is the darling
of the great lord of Hing,
the other's man, T'an's viscount is.

Hand soft as a blade of grass,
a skin like cream, neck like the glow-worm's light,

her teeth as melon seeds,
a forehead neat as is a katydid's,
her brows and lids, as when you see her smile
or her eyes turn, she dimpling the while,
clear white, gainst black iris.

Tall she came thru the till'd fields to the town,
her quadriga orderly
that four high stallions drew
with scarlet-tasselled bits, and pheasant tails
in woven paravant.
Thus to the court, great officers, retire,
and let our noble Lord assuage his fire.

Ho tumbles north, tumultuous, animate,
forking the hills;
sturgeon and gamey trout
swim and leap out
to spat of nets and flap of flat fish-tails,
with Kiang dames' high hair-dos flashing bright
above the cortège's armèd might.

IV
PEDLAR

Hill-billy, hill-billy, come to buy
silk in our market, apparently?
toting an armful of calico.

Hill-billy, hill-billy, not at all
but come hither to plot my fall,
offering cloth for raw silk and all,
till I went out over the K'i
to Tun Mount, in fact, quite willingly,
and then I asked for a notary.
I said: It's O.K. with me,
we could be spliced autumnally,
                              be not offended.

Autumn came, was waiting ended?
I climbed the ruin'd wall, looked toward Kuan pass.
On the Kuan frontier no man was.
I wept until you came,
trusted your smiling talk.   One would.

You said the shells were good and the stalks all clear.
You got a cart
and carted off me and my gear.

> Let doves eat no more mulberries
> While yet the leaves be green,
> And girls play not with lustful men,
> Who can play and then explain,
>   for so 'tis usèd,
>   and girls be naught excusèd.

The mulberry tree is bare,
yellow leaves float down thru the air,
Three years we were poor,
now K'i's like a soup of mud,
the carriage curtains wet, I ever straight
and you ambiguous
with never a grip between your word and act.

Three years a wife, to work without a roof,
up with the sun and prompt to go to bed,
never a morning off. I kept my word.
You tyrannize, Brothers unaware,
if told would but grin and swear
(with truth, I must confess):
If I'm in trouble, well, I made the mess.

"Grow old with you," whom old you spite,
K'i has its banks and every swamp an edge.
Happy in pig-tails, laughed to hear your pledge,
sun up, sun up, believing all you said,
who in your acts reverse
(as a matter of course)
all that you ever said
and for the worse,
an end.

V
SEHNSUCHT, LONG POLES   59

Slim poles to fish in the K'i
but no bamboo long
enough to reach you
save in a song;

To left is Yüan Spring,
to right, the K'i;
a girl flows out
leaving her family.

K'i River to right
at left flows Yüan Spring,
slow flash of a quiet smile, jangling
of the stones at your belt.

Oars (and are they of juniper?) lift and fall in the K'i
in my mind's eye the pine boat swerves
as I drive in the park
to quiet my nerves.

VI
WOLF

Feeble as a twig,
with a spike so big
in his belt, but know us he does not.
     Should we melt
at the flap of his sash ends?

Feeble as a gourd stalk (epidendrum)
to walk with an out-size ring
at his belt (fit for an archer's thumb
that might be an archer's,
as if ready for archery
which he is not)
we will not, I think, melt,
(complacency in its apogee)
at the flap of his sash ends.

VII

Wide, Ho?
A reed will cross its flow;
Sung far?
One sees it, tip-toe.

Ho strong?
The blade of a row-boat cuts it so soon.
Sung far? I could be there
(save reverence) by noon

                    (did I not venerate
                    Sung's line and state.) *

             VIII   62

Baron at arms,
ten-cubit halbard to war is
in the front rank
of the king's forays
                    driving, driving:

Eastward,
Eastward.
Why oil my hair, that's like a bush flying,
Or pile it high
If he come not forbye.

Rain, oh rain,
in drought's time,
Or the bright sun quickens;
and a rhyme in my thought of him:
For sweetness of the heart
the head sickens.

How shall I find forgetting-grass
to plant when the moon is dark
that my sorrow would pass
or when I speak my thought? Alas.

             IX
             (STRIP—TEASE?)   63

K'i dam, prowls fox,
a heart 's to hurt
and someone 's there has got no skirt.

* Said to be by the divorced wife of Huan of Sung, after her son's accession, decorum
forbidding her to return to court.

By the K'i's deep on the prowl;
got no belt on, bless my soul.

Tangle-fox by K'i bank tall:
who says: got no clothes at all?

X

Gave me a quince, a beryl my cover,
not as a swap, but to last forever.

For a peach thrown me, let green gem prove:
exchange is nothing, all time 's to love.

For a plum thrown me
I made this rhyme
with a red "ninth-stone"
to last out all time.

BOOK 6. SONGS OF WANG
Breviora (Lieder) of Kingsland
or the Royal Domain

I
THRU THE SEASONS
"O thou man." Thos. Hardy in
Under the Greenwood Tree

Black millet heeds not shaggy sprout,
Aimless slowness, heart's pot scraped out,
Acquaintance say: Ajh, melancholy!
Strangers: he hunts, but why?
> Let heaven's far span, azure darkness,
> declare what manner of man this is.

Black millet heeds not the panicled
ear in the forming.
Aimless slowness, heart in dead daze,
Acquaintance say: Ajh, melancholy!
Strangers say: he hunts, but why?
> Let heaven's far span, azure darkness,
> declare what manner of man this is.

Black millet recks not the heavy ears
of the temple grain.
Aimless slowness, heart choked with grief.
Acquaintance say: Ajh, melancholy!
Strangers say: he hunts, but why.
                    Let heaven's far span, azure darkness,
                    declare what manner of man this is.*

                              "Tous je connais"
                                          Villon.

ALITER

From the commentary:
"Where once was palace
now is straggling grain."

Straggling millet, grain in shoot,
aimless slowness, heart's pot scraped out,
acquaintance say: He is melancholy;
Strangers: what is he hunting now?

              Sky, far, so dark.
              "This, here, who, how?"

Straggling millet, grain on the stalk,
walking aimless, heart drunk with grief.
Acquaintance say: Ah, melancholy.
Strangers: What is he hunting now?

              Sky, slate, afar,
              "This man, who, how?"

Straggling millet, grain heavy in ear
aimless slowness, choking in heart
my acquaintance say: How melancholy.
Strangers: What is he hunting now?

              Sky never near:
              "This, here, who, how?" †

* According to tradition, a lament on the overgrown site of the old capital. Including parts of the commentary one would get the refrain:
              By the far heaven's dark canopy
              What manner of man hath wrought this misery?

† The heaven is far off, there is here a human agency. One very often comes round to old Legge's view, after devious by-paths.

He's to the war
for the duration;
Hens to wall-hole,
beasts to stall,
shall I not remember
him at night-fall?

He's to the war
for the duration,
fowl to their perches,
cattle to byre;
is there food enough;
drink enough
by their camp fire?

What a man! with a bamboo flute calls me out
to gad about and be gay

> moreover!

What a man with a feather fan calls me out
to gad about to the stage play

> and then some!

IV

**Troops transferred from
one mountain area to another**

Rapids float no fagot here
nor can she guard Shen frontier.

> Heart, O heart, when shall I home?

Ripples float no thorn-pack thru
nor will she fight by us in Fu.

> Heart, O heart, when shall I home?

Freshets float no osier here
nor can she guard Hü frontier.

> Heart, O heart, when shall I home?

Ripples break no fagot band.*

* If at head waters, can receive no message token by water-post; cf/the messages sent
in this way in the Tristan legend.

Dry grass, in vale:
                    "alas!

"I met a man, I
                met
                        a man.

"Scorched, alas, ere it could grow."
A lonely girl pours out her woe.

"Even in water-meadow, dry."
Flow her tears abundantly,
                    Solitude 's no remedy.

Rabbit goes soft-foot, pheasant 's caught,
I began life with too much élan,
Troubles come to a bustling man.
                    "Down Oh, and give me a bed!"

Rabbit soft-foot, pheasant 's in trap,
I began life with a flip and flap,
Then a thousand troubles fell on my head,
                    "If I could only sleep like the dead!"

Rabbit goes soft-foot, pheasant gets caught.
A youngster was always rushin' round,
Troubles crush me to the ground.
                    I wish I could sleep and not hear a sound.

ALITER

Ole Brer Rabbit watchin' his feet,
Rabbit net 's got the pheasant beat;
            When I was young and a-startin' life
            I kept away from trouble an' strife
But then, as life went on,
Did I meet trouble?
                    Aye, my son;
Wish I could sleep till life was done.

Vine over vine along the Ho,
thru the vine-clad wilderness I go
so far from home to call a stranger "Dad,"
       who will not hear.

Vine over vine by edges of the Ho,
thru the tangled vines I go
so far to come to seek a stranger's care
Should I say "mother" to some stranger there?

Vine over vine upon the brinks of Ho,
entangled vine
so far from home. Say "brother" to some stranger?
      Where none 's mine.

VIII

TAEDIUM

Plucking the vine leaves, hear my song:
"A day without him is three months long."

Stripping the southernwoods, hear my song:
"A day without him is three autumns long."

Reaping the tall grass hear my song:
"A day without him 's three years long."

IX

In stately chariot, robes a green flare,
think of you?
      Do I dare?

In creaking car of state and fleecy gown,
as a cornelian bright in panoply,
Think of you?
      I dare not so high.

So different a house in life, and then to lie
in the one earthen cell, unendingly.
And my sincerity?
      As the sun's eye.

Hemp on hill,
tell me, pray:
What keeps young Tsy Tsie away?

On mid slope
wheat grows fine,
Why doesn't Tsy Kuo come to dine?

There blows a plum on yonder hill
who wants those young bucks for her own.
Shall I give up my girdle stone?

BOOK 7. SONGS OF CHENG

"Banish the songs of Cheng."
K'ung, the Anthologist

K'ung-fu-tsy seems to have regarded the tunes
to these verses as a species of crooning
or boogie-woogie.

I

Live up to your clothes,
        we'll see that you get new ones.
You do your job,
        we'll bring our best food to you 'uns.

If you're good as your robes are good
We'll bring you your pay and our best food.

Nothing too good, bigosh and bigob
For a bureaucrat who will really
                        attend to his job.

Hep-Cat Chung, 'ware my town,
don't break my willows down.
The trees don't matter
but father's tongue, mother's tongue
            Have a heart, Chung,
                    it's awful.

Hep-Cat Chung, don't jump my wall
nor strip my mulberry boughs,
The boughs don't matter
But my brothers' clatter!
   Have a heart, Chung,
      it's awful.

Hep-Cat Chung, that is *my* garden wall,
Don't break my sandalwood tree.
The tree don't matter
But the subsequent chatter!
   Have a heart, Chung,
      it's awful.

III

Shu goes hunting, no one stays
in the town's lanes and by-ways
or if they do
there's not a he-man there like Shu.

Shu 's after game, no one at table or bottle now
to eat or drink, or if they do
they are not a patch on Shu.

Shu 's in the wild field, there 's no hitched horse in town;
though if you might
find someone driving there
'twere no such knight.

IV

Shu 's to the field, the reins of his double team
seem silken strands;
His outer stallions move
as in a pantomime. Thru thicket and marsh
flare beaters' fires.
Stript to the waist he holds a tiger down
for the Duke's smile and frown:
   "This once, but not again.
   I need such men."

Shu 's to the hunt,
his wheel-bays pull strong.
The other pair are as twin geese a-wing.
He comes to marsh, the beaters' fires flash out.
Good archer and good driver to control,
The envy of all, be it to drive or shoot.

Again to hunting, now with the grays,
Pole pair show even head,
Outer pair like a hand outspread.
Shu to the break,
thru thicket swamp flare the fires.
Then driving slow,
Quiver set down, shoot comes to end.
Envy of all, he cases his bow.

V

MANOEUVRES

"D'un air bonasse."

Vlaminck

79

Ts'ing men in P'eng
having a fling,
staff car, tasselled spears, snorting
horses cavorting,
                    by Ho!

Ts'ing men in Siao, staff cars clank,
one spear higher than tother,
as they meander
                    by Ho bank.

Ts'ing men in Chou,
drivers, guards, and a left turn, right draw,
space, a place,
as we observe the commander's
                            affable face.

VI   80

Lamb-skin for suavity, trimmed and ornate,
But a good soldier who will get things straight;

39   I·7   SONGS OF CHENG

Note that lamb coat, fleecy to leopard cuff,
a dude, but he knows his stuff.

Who gave three buttons meant:
This chap 's no mere ornament.

I plucked your sleeve by the way, that you should pause.
Cast not an old friend off without cause.

That a hand's clasp in the high road could thee move:
Scorn not an old friend's love.

"Cock crow!" she says.
He says: "'Tis dark."
"Up, sir," she says,
"Up, see, get out
and shoot the geese that be flyin' about."

"You shoot, I cook, that is as it should be,
eat, drink, grow old in mutual amity,
guitars and lutes in clear felicity.

I knew you'd come, by the girdle stone,
I to obey for the second one.
Three stones at a girdle be
Signs of returned felicity."

In chariot like an hibiscus flower at his side
ready to ride and go, with gemmèd belt
Kiang's eldest frail and beauty of the town, our capital;

Like an hibiscus spray to walk with him,
to sway, to hover
as that petal'd flower, with sound of pendants
swinging at her waist, Kiang's eldest loveliness,
say in that sound is her true nature traced,

Nor shall effacèd be,
once known, from memory.

1·7 SONGS OF CHENG

X
THE ADORNED BUT IMMATURE GALLANT

On mount doth noble ilex grow
and marsh weed in the lowland low.

> 'Tis not Tsy-tu doth now appear;
> No man, but a boy perks here.

High pine on hill,
in swamp the dragon flower,

> Not lovers' twilight this,
> but the children's hour.

XI

Withered, withered, by the wind's omen,
a state lost for the soft mouth of a woman;

What the wind hath blown away,
can men of Cheng rebuild it in a day.*

ALITER

Withered, withered at the winds' call,
Uncles you lead, I follow you all;

Withered, withered, as the wind floats,
You pipe, my uncles, I but follow your notes.

XII

So he won't talk to me when we meet?
Terrible!
> I still can eat.

So clever he won't even come to dinner;
Well, beds are soft,
> and I'm no thinner.

* Where the winds blow, withered leaves must.
   Folk under overlords are as blown dust.
L. and K. completely at loggerheads. Following Mao the meaning would be: The prince,
overborne by his ministers, ironizes.

XIII

Be kind, good sir, and I'll lift my sark
and cross the Chen to you,
But don't think you are the only sprig
                  in all the younger crew.

Think soft, good sir, and I'll lift my sark
and cross the Wei to you;
But play the pretentious ass again, and
                  some other young captain will do.

XIV

88

A handsome lad stood in the lane,
Alas, I asked him to explain.

A rich boy came for me to the hall
and I wasn't ready. How should it befall?
                  Who wants a lady?

Here in my hidden embroideries
with a plain dress over them down to my knees,
Junior or elder, harness and come,
come with a wagon and cart a girl home.

Top and skirt of embroideries
covered in plain silk down to my knees,
Junior or elder, harness and come,
bring on your wagon and take a girl home.

XV

89

East gate's level stretch of land,
madder on bank there, easy to hand,
so near his home, and he so far.

By the east gate chestnuts grow
over garden walls so low,
There I ever think of thee,
and thou comest ne'er to me.

XVI

"As on the last day of the moon"

Cold wind, and the rain,
cock crow, he is come again,
    my ease.

Shrill wind and the rain
and the cock crows and crows,
I have seen him, shall it suffice
    as the wind blows?

Wind, rain and the dark
as it were the dark of the moon,
What of the wind, and the cock's never-ending cry;
Together
again
he and I.

XVII
THE STUDENT'S BLUE
COLLAR OR LAPEL

Blue, blue collar, my heart's delight,
I can't come out,
Why shouldn't you write?

Blue, blue sash, heart's misery.
I cannot come out, but you might come to me.

You swish about
between gates of the towered wall,
So far, no wrong.
One day without you
is three months long.

XVIII

Dashing waters untie not
the knot that binds a thorn fagot.
Elder and younger brothers we
in bonds of so small family,
Trust not men's idle tales
who use words to hide their thought.

Splashing unties no fagot bound,
elder and younger brothers we;
I say: trust not their perfidy.

                    XIX

At the great gate to the East
Mid crowds
be girls like clouds
who cloud not my thought in the least.

                    Gray scarf and a plain silk gown
                    I take delight in one alone.

Under the towers toward the East
be fair girls like flowers to test,

                    Red bonnet and plain silk gown
                    I take delight with one alone.

                    XX

Mid the bind-grass on the plain
that the dew makes wet as rain
I met by chance my clear-eyed man,
                    then my
                    joy began.

Mid the wild grass dank with dew
lay we the full night thru,
                    that clear-eyed man and I
                    in mutual felicity.

                    XXI
                    SAY IT WITH PEONIES

Chen and Wei
flow thereby
                    touching together,
Man and girl, girl and man
                    to pluck valerian:

"The play?" says she.
"Seen it." says he.
"If so, let's go
Over Wei
pleasantly."

Playing there, girls and men
Prescribe this mutual medicine.

Chen and Wei in alacrity
as pampas blades a-gleam
by bank and stream
come girls and a throng of officers.

She says: "Have you seen . . . ?"
He says: "I been."
"Let's again." Over Wei
Pleasantly,
Ready girl, ready man
offer mutual medicine.

BOOK 8. THE OFTEN MILDLY
SATIRICAL VERSES OF TS'I

NONDUM ORTO JUBARE.
Alba belingalis   96

"Cock's crow'd. The courtiers are all
crowding the hall."
Cock hasn't, she lies
but one hears some blue flies.

"East's bright. Court's met."
East's not, but the waning moon *
sends up some light.

* Waning moon,
moon is about to set.

"Flies fly high, but also hum,
'Twere sweet to dream, by side, but knights
who walk from court assembly also talk and might even rage
at innocent
concubinage."

"That turn 'll get her." I said.
We were loafing about under Nao,
each in his hunting gig
after a brace of wild pig;
You bowed and replied: "Yours, better!"

"Some cut." I said.
We had come to the meet at Dog Hill,
two boar for the kill. You said,
with a bow: "And yours, now!"

We met on the south slope of Nao,
wolves the game this time,
the exchange of the same lightness,
save that you said bowing: "Majesterial!"
a huntsman not to be outdone in politeness.

He waited me by our gate-screen,
                    come by, come by.
His ear-plugs shone so florally,
                    come by,
on white silk tassels airily,
                    come by, come by.

He came straight in to our court-yard,
                    come by, come by.
His ear-plugs flamed so fiery,
                    come by,
on silken thread like greenery,
                    come by.

He stopped not till he reached the hall,
                    come by, come by.
The yellow tassels airily
held two topaze right royally,
                    come by, come by.

                IV
                TOWN LIFE   99

Sun's in the East,
her loveliness
Comes here
To undress.

Twixt door and screen
at moon-rise
I hear
Her departing sighs.

                V   100

Still dark,
mistaking a kilt for a coat
upside down:
                "To the Duke, sir, since ..."

It was not yet light,
mistaking a coat for a kilt,
down for up,
                and to audience!

Break thru the close garden fence
with staring eyes, a fool tries.
Milord 's lost all sense of tense
night, day, audience,
day, night,
and no time ever right.

                VI   101

South Mount soaring, cock fox sly,
Lu Road wide open as Miss Ts'i went to bride.
I said, to bride.
                Put it aside.

Five kinds of vine-rope shoes
by twos, cap-strings are mated.
And Lu Road was wide, when Miss Ts'i, as stated
went to bride, settled and fixed,
                    Why push betwixt.

How sow hemp? Hemp goes by furrows,
formal weddings fix tomorrows.
          A girl is placed by those who breed her,
          Would you now still cuddle and feed her?

How 's kindling split?
By axe, and the fit
tool to arrange a marriage with decencies,
is the broker who sees
to the details and formalities.
And you'd move her?
Now the whole job is settled and over?

VII
"Their eyes are in the ends of the Earth."   102

Field not too great a field
lest weeds outproud thy grain;
nor of foreign affairs
lest 'ou break under strain.

Field not too great a field
lest the overgrowth break thee,
nor foreigners
lest worry unmake thee.

The tufted babe
that wriggles in thy lap,
ere thou art ware
will wear a grown man's cap.

VIII   103

With sound of the hounds, black hounds,
he is riding the bounds, a tall man, a real man.

"Ting-a-ding" sound the hounds, black hounds
on double ring.

A sporting man's fling, triple ring
to his hounds, when a man
thinks of his hunting.

(Some men think of the game or else
give attention to rings, hair-dos and bells.)

The wicker of the weir is broke,
loose fish are out again
as the Lady of Ts'i comes home
with a cloud in her train.

The wicker of the weir is broke
as ex-Miss Ts'i comes home again,
luce and perch be broken out
as many as drops of rain.

The wicker of the weir is broke
and these fish make a very great clatter.
The Lady of Ts'i comes home with a train,
all of them loose as water.*

LA MADONE DES WAGONS–LITS

On comes her car with a rattle-de-bang,
woven leather like cinnabar,
Loose, loose, a flaming star,
id est, Miss Ts'i shooting the moon
to Lu,
      to Lu,
             started at sunset, none too soon.

With a black flash of quadrigas
and the multitude of her chariots,
double teams matched, smooth-oiled reins,
Lu Road stretching across the plains.

Full be the waters of Wen
as we hear the whang of marching men,
Miss Ts'i and Lu Road we see
both wider than all liberality.

* Legge says the satire is against her son the Duke of Lu for not keeping the dowager
in order. Karlgren dissents. "Loose Fish," usual term for unattached males.

Across Wen water churning mud
a herd of travellers in flood
and, loose on Lu Road, Miss Ts'i
showing compassion abundantly.

XI

"An ater an albus" . . .

Catullus

106

Compleat, alas, and prosperous,
profile'd and tall "to lower is as to raise."
His fine eyes blaze,
Clever of foot and great in archery.

Competent, alas, and of wide fame,
a dark pellucid eye;
Focussed in equity,
can shoot all day and never miss the dot,
        a nephew, a spread nephew, certainly.

Competent, alas, and of winning grace,
clearly with naught to learn *in feminis*
or in the dance and courtly pantomime,
bull's-eye each time,
four arrows on the dot:
        could he block civil war,
        or should he not?

BOOK 9. SONGS OF NGWEI
(Under Tsin domination, presumably,
the new ruling class from seven
points of view.)

107

Thin fibre shoes 'gainst frost,
At soft hands' cost a girl can make her clothes
or ply the needle with those same hands
to make her goodman's stiff belt and bands.

Goodman? or mean? we mean
good to accumulate and accumulate,
noted of late at her left hand
on formal occasions, meticulous
with an ivory pin in a belt *
which cramps him, we mean
the tightening has an inner cause

(if you take not the pin's point, but ours.)

II
ENCROACHMENT
"Families who use ice, do not etc."

                                    Ta Hic   108

To gather sorrel
in swamplands of Fen,
is a suitable act for local men,
but for a resplendent officer
who moves in charge of a ducal car?

Fen has one grove of mulberry trees
Fen folk were wont to use
till such a flowery officer,
a "button man," came to administer
and have charge of the public roads.

By one crook of the Fen ox-lip grows
that Fen folk once gathered to ease their woes
till we got such a gem of an officer
of the Duke's household,
of the kind some dukes prefer.

III
JE BOIS DANS MON VERRE
                                                             109

Garden peach, in a dish ere long (my own)
as my worry goes into song.
Strangers say: "The scholar is proud.
Others fit in. Why 's he so loud?"
Those who know me, plumb not my thought.

* Ivory pins or spikes carried in the belt for untying knots.

Garden blackberry (my own) made to eat,
a heart worries for the state of the State;
Strangers find me utterly wrong
because "other men get along."
Friends, finding me distraught,
Plumb not my thought.

(Who can plumb another man's thought?)

IV

I climb the knoll;
gaze to my father's land from the knoll's shade,
and he will be saying, praying:
                "That boy's on hard service
                dawn to sundown, no end.
                Let him care for the flag, as I could commend.
                So he return in the end."

I climb bald rock, eyes seek
my mother's house, and she:
                "No rest, my bairn,
                That his bones lie not in the waste."

I climb the ridge
look to my brother's stead,
and he:
                "The kid is abroad,
                a file filled,
                If only he doesn't get killed
                (and an eye on the flag.)"

V

In their ten-acre allotments, barons at ease
say: "These are surely our mulberry trees."

Outside their allotments, as I've heard tell,
they say just as calmly: ". . . and these as well."

VI
"SILK–DINE"
that is, in idleness

K'an, k'an, sandalwood
planks are good by Ho
on clear water we float their weight.

Men of state
nor sow nor reap
yet keep grain to fill three hundred markets;
never hunt nor hear dogs bark, yet
never lack
badger skins to cover the back.
And I could name
some courtyards filled with a total district's game,
 where they dine in milk-white silk
 (Idle food to the nobleman!)

K'an, k'an,
axes clank.
From oak to spoke,
we pile the planks by Ho bank,
steady as the waters flow.
They never sow nor reap
nor hunt, yet keep
grain as much as three hundred krores
and have yards full of young, hung wild boars
 to help 'em dine in milk-white silk
 (Idle food for the nobleman!)

K'an, k'an, trim
and bend a wheel-rim
by whirling water we pile the logs
on bank; they never hunt or run with the dogs,
nor sow, nor reap, yet keep
grain to fill up three hundred bins,
and when they would stuff their skins
in their court one never fails
to see a string of good fat quails.
 So they dine in milk-white silk.
 (Idle food for a nobleman.)

 VII
 RATS   113

RATS,
stone-head rats lay off our grain,
three years pain,
enough, enough, plus enough again.

More than enough from you, deaf you,
we're about thru and ready to go
where something will grow
untaxed.
Good earth, good sown,
and come into our own.

RATS,
big rats, lay off our wheat,
three years deceit,
and now we're about ready to go
to Lo Kuo, happy, happy land, Lo Kuo, good earth
where we can earn our worth.

RATS,
stone-head rats, spare our new shoots,
three years, no pay.
We're about ready to move away
to some decent border town.
Good earth, good sown,
and make an end to this endless moan.

BOOK 10. SONGS OF T'ANG
the northernmost part of the great
Tsin fief under the Chou dynasty.
Yao's country.

I   114

Cricket in hall, the year runs to its close,
Rejoice and now, ere sun and moon subtract.
Exceed no bound, think what thine office is;
      Enjoy the good, yet sink not in excess.
      Hereto is good knight's true attentiveness.

Cricket in hall, the year is on the wain.
The sun and moon defend no man's delight.
Stretch not thy wish, know where stands outerness,
Right man is light of foot in banquet rite.

Cricket's in hall, the killers' carts put by,
Rejoice and now, tho' suns be insolent.
Too-much sires woe, be mindful of thine extent.
        Enjoy the good yet sink not in excess,
        True scholar stands by his steadfastness.

Thorn-elm on mountain, white elm on slope,
the clothes you never wear,
carriages idle there
be another's fact or hope
        when you are dead, who now but mope.

Kao tree on crest, shrub in low-land,
dust in your courtly dancing place,
bells on rack and drums unlaced
shall be others' jollity
        when you've proved your mortality.

Terebinth stands high on the crest, chestnut in vale,
wine thou hast and lutes in array,
undrunk, unstruck today.
Who makest not carouse:
        another shall have thy house.*

Water dashing
on sharp-edged rocks;
silk robe and red lapel
followed to Wu
and saw Milord there,
                wasn't that a happy affair!

Swift water knocks
on the bright white rocks;
white silk robe and broidered axe
followed to Ku and saw the chief,
                who could say that was grief?

* Traditionally an admonition to Marquis Chao of Tsin, written between 744–738 B.C.

Water dashing
on white flare of stone;
We hear it is ordered and dare tell none.*

"Evviva la torre di Pisa!"   117

Oh, the pods keep a sproutin'
                upon the pepper tree,
the sprouts keep a risin'
and the big pods hangin' down,
the pods keep a growin'
                for a strong man on his own.

The big pods keep a hangin',
the sprouts keep a risin'
and the big pods hangin' down,
the new sprouts keep a growin'
                for a strong man on his own.†

V

TS'AN

the three stars of Orion   118

She says:
                I've tied the faggots round,
                Three stars are in the sky,
                        a night, a night,
                to see my man, and hold him pleasantly.

                Now I've bundled up the grass,
                Three stars rise o'er the hill,
                        a night to meet,
                        a night to meet,
                        by luck, not by our will.

* Tradition that this concerns the conspiracy of Ch'eng-shy against Chao, Marquis of
Tsin; commentators at loggerheads as to its bearing: pro-rock, pro-water, loyalty to legal
insignia, warning, irony, incitement, taunt to Ch'eng-shy who had illegally assumed the
insignia. Which wd/ come to: We hear you have the appointment (from heaven) but
fear to proclaim (kao) it openly. 744–738 B.C. The obscurity undoubtedly intentional.
† Traditionally refers to rising power of Huan-Shu, co-rebel with Ch'eng-shy.

He says:

> Now I've bound the thorns together,
> Three stars above the door
> have brought me to tie with such a lass
> as never I saw before.

VI

The pear tree stands alone, a-gleam with leaf,
I walk alone, my grief,
among men upon the road, none of my father's breed
                lifts load, shares aim.

The pear tree stands alone, so green in leaf,
Bowed and alone, my grief
where no man shares my name
fraternal upon the road
                lifts load, shares aim.

VII
(Meaning wholly conjectural)

Lamb-skin coat and a leopard cuff
goes on living beneath my roof.

There are others, I've been told
and this one is gettin' old.

Askin' and askin', now I hear
others are called and might appear
with a lambskin coat and leopard trim
although I am fond of him.*

VIII
PAO
That carrion crow has advantage.

Buzzards on oak, after neat flight,
King's work is never to slight,
Now we cannot tend our grain
What shall sustain father or mother, heaven say:
Is this our crime? shall we home again?

* Legge follows commentators who interpret it as complaint against a bad governor, personally liked. My translation probably wrong, and others' no better.

Buzzards fly and nest in thorns,
thick the thorns as the king's affairs.
Neglect of grain no man spares.
How shall a father and mother eat
with this deficient grain supply?
Shall the far archèd heaven defend
mankind from such an end?

Buzzards from sky come down mid mulberries,
In king's affairs is no ease,
As test?
Shall father or mother see
rice or spiked-grain harvest?

Such darkness the archèd heaven brings
as the common order of things.

IX   122

'Tis to lack seven robes
lacking thine,
which gift could a peace define.

As if losing the sixth coat
(if he lack thine)
leave peace remote.

X
At the road's bend
dare say he'd make a
nice gentleman-friend.   123

Lonely pear tree by the way side,
How shall I for my true-love provide?

Dare say he'd agree, but how feed him?

Russet pear at bend of the way,
Dare say he'd come play, but . . .

True love won't feed him.

ALBA

Creeper grows over thorn,
bracken wilds over waste, he is gone,
Gone, I am alone.

Creeper overgrows thorn,
bracken spreads over the grave, he is gone,
Gone, I am alone.

The horn pillow is white like rice,
the silk shroud gleams as if with tatters of fire.
In the sunrise I am alone.

A summer's day,
winter's night, a hundred years
and we come to one house together.

Winter's day, summer's night,
each night as winter night,
each day long as of summer,
                but at last to the one same house.

XII

"Pick ling! Pick ling! on Shou-Yang's crest!"
Such words, a mere mare's-nest,
                would not stir credulity
                yet you believe the worst of me.
If you swallow such nonsense now
When will you find a way, or how?

"Go for thistles to South-Head's base."
Would you try in any case?
                Indeed you would not, why and how
                can you swallow such nonsense now?

"And for mustard? Shou-Yang's east side."
Would you try it, or have you tried?
                Tell me truly, who but a fool
                Believes such silly tales out of school.

BOOK 11. SONGS OF TS'IN
Feudal state from 897–221, rising to
dynasty after Chou. As the Chou
capital moved eastward, Ts'in subject
to wild infiltration from the West.

I 126

Chariots, rank on rank
with white-fronted horses;
You'd see Milord?
                    Eunuchs are bosses.

Terebinth on the hill, chestnuts in valley;
Once you're inside, there are lutes in each alley.
                    Delight, delight
                    and the long night
                                        coming.

Mulberries on the crest,
willows in marsh-land valley,
                    drum-beat and shamisan,
                                        dally, dally,
                    Death's up the alley.

II
WINTER HUNT 127

His sports-car leads with the iron-grays,
six reins are in his hand
and behind come all the hunt
to follow at his command,

Now boars rush from underbrush,
strong against spear,
young pigs of the year;
and the Duke's voice clear:
                    "To the left,
                    by the bounds,
                    pull out the hounds."

Hallo and Hark
then to North Park

double teams
neat in their rounds
with the tinkling sounds
of bells, and the long and short-nosed hounds.

III

So have I seen him in his service car
who now in war afar,
five bands on the curving pole, side shields and silver'd trace,
bright mats and bulging hub;
dapple and white-foot pace
into my thought. I see him neat as jade
in service shack, and in my thought confused.

Great dapples held, and by six reins restrained,
black-maned,
the darker pair outside,
locked dragon shield and silver-ringèd rein
before my thought again
who now by border wall
moves suave as once in hall.

Team in an even block, gilt trident-haft
with silver-basèd butt, and emboss'd shields,
bow-case of tiger's fell, graved lorica;
the bows are bound to laths inside their case;
Shall he not fill my thought,
                by day, by night,
whose mind and act are right,
whose fame, delight?

IV
PHANTOM

129

Dark, dark be reed and rush,
the white dew turns to frost;
                what manner of man is this?
                        lost?

        Gin I rin up,
        Gin I go down,
        Up stream heavy, there he'd be
        In mid water distantly.

Chill, chill be the reeds,
the white dew not yet dry;
        What manner of man is he
        under the hanging bank?

        Up stream heavily.
        gin I swim down,
        on tufted isle
        distantly.

Ever falls dew on bright reeds.
        What manner of thing is he
        who seems to be there on the marge

        Up stream, to the West, at large?
        Hard to go up, to swim, tho' he seem
        there on the isle, mid-stream.

V
The outdoor chief
establishes court

On South sky-line, white fir and plum
So the Prince come,
        fox fur for broidery,
        ruddy of face,
        true lord, true race.

On South Mountain, vale and aisle
Tale of the hall he reared meanwhile,
Whose blue-black robe showed double axe displayed.
Hear, at his belt "tsiang-tsiang" of the pendant jade.*
        To whom longevity
        and fame always in memory.

* The "tsiang-tsiang" is onomatopoeia but the lines could also be rendered:
    Saith ever: "shall and shall";
        never: "oblivion."

THE THREE SHAY BROTHERS
Funeral sacrifice for Duke Mu, 621 B.C.

Ever unstill, cross, cross,
yellow wings come to the thorn.

Who? with Duke Mu?
Shay Yen-Si. Who?
Shay Yen-Si, pick of an hundred men, shook at the grave's edge then.

Dark heaven, you take our best men,
An hundred; to have him again.

Ever unstill, cross, the yellow birds
come to mulberry boughs.

Who? with Duke Mu?
Shay Chung-Hang. Who?
Shay Chung-Hang who'd block an hundred men
Moaned at the grave's brink then.

Dark heaven, you take our best men,
An hundred to have him again.

Ever unstill, cross, cross,
The yellow wings come to the thorn,

Who? with Duke Mu?
Shay K'ien-Hu, who could hold an hundred men,
Shook at the grave's brink then.

Dark heaven, you wipe out our best men.
We'd give an hundred
To have him again.

VII
"Long wind, the dawn wind"

Falcon gone to the gloom
and the long wind of the forest
Forgetting the children I bore you,
          North, North?

Thick oak on mount, six grafted pears in the low,
                    Whither, whither
                    North, north
                    forgetful so?

Plum trees of the mountain,
Peach blossoms of the plain
                    Whither, whither?
I am drunk with the pain.

                    VIII   133

What! No clothes?
Share my cloak, at the king's call
spear, lance and all
prepare
                    and advance
                    with axes, together.

What! no clothes?
My underwear is just your size.
Levies arise,
at the king's call
we rise all
                    with lances and halbards, together.

What! no clothes?
Take my spare kilt. Shine mail-coat and axe!
                    Lift we our packs
                    and out together.

                    IX   134

With him to say good-bye
To the north banks of the Wei,
                    Uncle, my uncle,
I bless thy ways
I give thee four bays
                    for thy car, at departing.

My thought within is deeper, uncle my own.
Take this jasper for girdle stone,
                    departing.

Alas, in Hia's house
where we made great carouse
Naught's now to spare.

The old tree bears no fruit
                    for Milord's heir.

Once four great courses were
set for each visitor,
all different. And all now different here,

The old tree bears no fruit
                    for Milord's heir.

65   I·11   SONGS OF TS'IN

SONGS OF THREE SMALL STATES
AND OF PIN
DUKE LIU'S OLD CAPITAL

BOOK 12. SONGS OF CH'EN

!

On Yüan hill, mutable, affable, candid,
but held of no account.

(Fluid as water that all tones reflects
of ten-day passion that no man respects.)

Under that hill to stand
tapping a hand-drum, waving an egret's feather,

Tapping an earthen pot on Yüan Road,
winter or summer, man
you weigh as much as your load:

the egret fan.

II

HILARE DIE

White elm at East Gate,
Bent Hill's oaks are tall,
Middle Sir's daughter
dances under them all.

Grain dawn for the errand,
we see "South Lady" race
her hemp unspun
to dance in the market place.

Grain dawn for going
till over the cauldron's edge
we see you as the Sun's flower;
grant we hold pepper in pledge.*

* A ritual dance, conjecturally, for solar fecundation.

Neath a patched door-flap,
no man to hurry me,
a spring of fresh water
and none to worry me.

There be bream that swim not in Ho;
Kiang girls of Ts'i
                    but others also.

More streams than Ho give fish
Tsy girls of Sung
                    be not the only dish.

There be bream that swim not in Ho;
Kiang-of-Ts'i girls
                    but others also.

More streams than Ho give fish,
Tsy-of-Sung girls be not the only dish.

IV
THE THIRD DAUGHTER OF KI

Soak hemp in East Moat, can't go wrong,
By East Gate 's a girl who will answer a song.

You can limber the thickest hemp in that situation,
and pass the time in polite conversation
                    with Miss Ki the 3rd/

Soak mat-grass by East Gate moat,
Miss Ki the 3rd/ is no flash in the pan, Sir,
But a young lady, and pretty,
                    who knows the answers.

V
RENDEZ–VOUS MANQUÉ

Neath East Gate willows
'tis good to lie.
She said:
        "this evening."
        Dawn 's in the sky.

Neath thick willow boughs
        'twas for last night.
Thick the close shade there.
        The dawn is axe-bright.

Thorns by the Campo Santo gate
need axe, and so does he, as most men know,
whose knowledge puts no end to his misdeeds.

Owls perch on cemetery trees,
plum trees, indeed, and hoot
and so do I, as were a warning and that gets no ear.
When he's knocked flat, he may hear.

ALITER

You can take an axe to the jujube trees
that clog the gates of cemeteries,
but to deal with this dirty cuss,
by courtesy only, anonymous?

To know is not to make an end
of his old habits, but of his friend.

Owl sits moody by graveyard gate
on the plum tree, to tell him to do this, that and t'other.
After he's down he may start to bother.

Magpies nest on the mound,
Sweet grass on higher ground,
        Who has lured my love away?
                My wound!

Tiles on the temple path,
The high bank hath
many a blossom still.
        Who was it lured my love away?
                My wound!

The erudite moon is up, less fair than she
who hath tied silk cords about
                    a heart in agony,
She at such ease
                    so all my work is vain.

My heart is tinder, and steel plucks at my pain
so all my work is vain,
                    she at such ease
                    as is the enquiring moon.

A glittering moon comes out
less bright than she the moon's colleague
that is so fair,
                    of yet such transient grace,
at ease, undurable, so all my work is vain
                    torn with this pain.*

THE DIVERSIVE

Why to the broken forest?
He follows the Summer South,
He drives not to the broken forest
                    But to Hia Nan's mouth.

"Harness my team of horses, harness and say:
'We go to the plain past Chu Ye.'
That'll help me, and help the colts thru
to breakfast in Chu." †

Marsh bank, lotus rank
                    and a ladye;
Heart ache and to lie awake
                    and a-fevered.

* A few transpositions but I think the words are all in the text.
† Legge says: a satire on Duke Ling's intrigue with Hia Nan. I take it with play on
meaning of her name "Summer South."

Marsh edge, valerian in sedge
>   and a ladye;
Hard head she hath.
I lie a-bed
>   afflicted.

Marsh bank, lotus rank,
>   a ladye,
straight as an altar stone her loveliness,
I lie in restlessness
>   all the night
>   comfortless.

ALITER

Graceful as acorus or lotus flower
what dame in bower
plagues me to wake from sleep?
I sweat from every vein.

As marsh hath rush or sharp valerian,
Tall formal beauty, and mid-heart my lack!

Marsh bank hath acorus to sway and flare,
Shall lily on lake compare
with a tall woman's loveliness
that though I wake or sleep
>   I turn and toss?

BOOK 13. SONGS OF KUEI

I   146

Fine clothes for sport
and slops in court
and your intent
is to show talent
>   for government?

Lamb's wool for sport,
fox fur in court and hall,
to me no festival.

Sure, the wool shines like fat
in the sun's rays; reflects the light
and is quite scintillant,
feathers of light in fact
                    to my heart's blight.

II
Sad 'tis to see good customs in neglect,
Our mourners now be no more circumspect.

Saw I a white cap now,
it were as music mid thorns,
                    Haro! the day.

Or a white robe?
Came such a robe in sight
methinks I would, outright,
go with the wearer miles upon his road.

Saw I white knee-pads decent misery
I'd know one man still feels and thinks as I.

III

Vitex in swamp ground,
branched loveliness,
would I could share that shrub's unconsciousness.

Vitex negundo, casting thy flowers in air,
thy joy to be, and have no family care.

Vitex in low marsh ground,
thy small fruit grows
in tenderness,
having no heavy house.

IV
THE KETTLE–DRUMS *

Not the wild wind
nor the roar of the chariots
                    But the ruin of Chou's way
                              breaks me.

* Vide Frobenius, the drums were made for temporary use by stretching the cover over the nomad's pots.

Not the storm's whirling
nor the war cars' surging
But the ruin of highways in Chou,

> and unpitied.

If a man can boil fish
let him wash out his cauldron,
If a man would home West
let him cherish this tone.

BOOK 14. SONGS OF TS'AO

I

POLONIUS ON OSTENTATION
(The banner-fly wears proper
mourning in season?)

150

Trappings as bright as wings of the banner-fly
give me concern,

> come back and live quietly.

Flashy your dress as light fly's moving wing
to my concern,

> could you come home?

Grub digs out of its hole to see and spy
snow-white the hemp of its panoply,
to my concern,

> could you come back and talk quietly.

II

OUTDOORS VERSUS THE COURT
(Conjecturally: country girl's
advice to the guardsman)

151

Marquis' yeoman, oh so brave
to lift lance or show signal stave,
but the person living at ease
has three hundred footmen with red pads on their knees.

Pelican on the dam
wets not a wing,
she 's less important than
her furnishing.

Pelican on the weir will not stir
even to dip its beak,
and she whom you seek
cares less than you for her.

South Mount, East Slope, you scarce can see thru the mist
when the dawn 's half alight.
Pleasant, yes, ready, yes,
the youngest girl has an appetite.

III
THE YOUNG IN NEWFANGLENESSE

Dove in this mulberry tree
feeds seven young untiringly;
Our lord, a unit of equity
hath heart of such constancy.

He keeps to his old nest,
the young wings flap
over the plum tree.

Silk sash and deer-spot cap,
still in the old precinct of mulberries;
they to the jujube now; the old eye ever on right,
no whimsies, the four corners ever in sight.

Dove in mulberry, young 'uns now try the hazel bough;
Call 'em the hazeleers;
He to the state gives form;
Sets norm:

Why not ten thousand years?
How not ten thousand years?

IV

Down from the spring the knife-sharp waters run
flooding the wolf-grass;
By night I wake and sigh
for Chou's lost majesty.
                    Chou 's down.

Cold waters flood and rot the sandal root;
By night I wake and sigh:
                              Chou 's down.

Chill waters seep milfoil in overflow;
By night I wake and weep that capital.

Millet rose thick, by mothering rain on soil;
Then were the Four States ruled by Earl Sün's toil.

BOOK 15. SONGS OF PIN

1

August sees the heat break.
In October we take our winter wear
gainst New Year's wind and March' cold air,
lacking serge of wool and hair
how 'ld we last till harvest time?

Third month: out the plows;
fourth: toe to field, childer and spouse
carry our snacks to the south sectors
where we prepare to meet the inspectors.

2

Sinketh the fiery sign neath the seventh moon;
ninth, we get clothes; when spring 'gins quicken
orioles in broom and bracken
cry to basket-bearing girls
trapsing about field-paths in Wei
to strip leaves from the mulberry;

as the slow days lengthen out
they'll to the southernwood, no doubt, and
mid the crowds some maids will sigh
for fear of the Duke's boys passing by
(we mean shrinking prospective brides
who'd prefer their home firesides.)

3

August moon marks the heat's edge,
September is for reed and sedge
when the silkworms start to hatch
we'll go twig the mulberry patch
with little axe and small hatchet
lop the splay boughs, to keep she-trees tight set.
So in August shrilleth shrike,
in September they'll spin belike
to make such yellow, stark red and black
as befits young lordling's back.

4

May is for grass seed,
June, Cicada's joy;
September, harvest, November to destroy
dead leaves,
Badger's in season when the year goes out,
wild-cat can make a young lord's coat.
In great hunts (March) that ready men for wars,
commons get piglets; nobles, the full-size boars.

5

June's green hopper moves a thigh,
"sedge-cock" wings it in July,
cricket 's a-field one month,
next, neath our eaves, and ere two more be sped,
he's over lintel, and crawls beneath thy bed.

Plug up the chinks, smoke out the rats,
block the north-lights, replaster wattle-slats
and tell the wife: the year draws to its close,
bide we at home the while, in full repose.

6

July 's to eat red plums, start on wild-vine.
Sunflower and bean in August pot combine;
strip, next, the dates, and neath November moon
take rice for saki that in spring eftsoon
shall keep old age and eyebrows from all need.

Eat melons in August, trim thy calabash,
then take in hemp seed. Trash,
thistles and fagots from any stinking tree
our farmers get as their gratuity.

7

Ninth month, beat hard
the space that was thy summer garden-yard
and in the tenth bring here field-sheaves to stack.
Early millet and late, hemp, beans nor wheat shall lack,
so tell the farm-hands: all the harvest 's in,
lets to our town, that indoor work begin.
Get grass by day, twist this by night to rope the thatch
lest any roof lack patch against the rain
whereneath to bide, till we sow next year's grain.

8

d'i̯ông, d'i̯ông (clash, crash) chop ice neath the second moon,
store it neath third, and in fourth month
when dawn's claw scratcheth sky
offer young lamb and leek roots pungently
if thou 'ldst have sheep to kill come next still frost,
asperge the yard for the twin-bottle feast
and with killed beasts then move processional
to lift great horn in the high ducal hall
and toast:

ten thousand years, Milord, to time's utmost.

II

Great horned owl, thieved my young!
Owl. Owl, raze not a house upsprung
from kindness, toil; we say the anointed young
are for pity.

2

Ere the sky was dark with rain
I set my trees to provide and tithe mulberries,
and with silken skein
bound door and lattice frame,
O you, down there,
who shall despise my name?

3

Hand that laboured, worn to the bone
clutching at thistles to build up the rent
and with a sore mouth,
shall I not have roof of my own?

4

Wings unfeathered, my tail unplumed,
a house in fragments, doomed,
shaken with wind and rain,
                  a-wash, afloat, *Aude me!* *

III
**GAG, said to have been used
in night attack to insure silence**
                                             156

From the long East Mount campaign
we came west, under a drizzle of rain
nor believed the news or their oaths,
but to be free of the gag and of army clothes.
Worms had filmed over the mulberry trees, under the stars
we guardsmen slept lonely, under our cars.

Homesick we went to the East Mountain,
We come now west again under a spatter of rain,
slogging along.
Gourds over the eaves,
sowbug in chamber, spiders ply
web over door;
what was once field is now forest thereby,
wild deer for cattle, take no fright
of the glow-worms' eerie light
that can be
aid to one's memory.

From the long East Mount campaign
came back under a sousing rain,
cranes loud on ant-hill to drown our consorts' weeping,
worn out with sweeping,
sprinkling and plugging the walls;

* The Duke of Chou against the uncles in the rebellion. *Mencius* II.i.IV, 3; *Shu* V.vi, 15.

levy comes home; bitter gourds over wood-pile
of chestnut boughs,
three years since the soldier has seen his house.

From the long East Mount campaign
we came west again under the rain.
Then the flash of an oriole's wing:
a new wife with dapple team come to meeting.
Her duenna has tied her formal sash, set
to the ninety rules of her etiquette;
piebal'd sorrels and bays a-dash to prove
a new love's glory — and no love
like an old love.

IV

Axes broken, hatchets lacking,
Eastward packing, the Duke of Chou gained
four states, and the Emperor reigned
over them all. He pitied our men,
Yet they were trained.

We have blunted our axes,
We lack work-tools,
Chou's Duke invades and rules as is fit
the four states of the East to their benefit;
Pity our men's condition,
his praise carries them on.

Axes broken, work-tools lacking,
Chou's Duke corrected
four states and connected
them all under one rule and test;
By his pity of fighting men
they now find rest.

V

How cut haft for an axe?

Who hacks
holds a haft.
To take a wife
properly
one gets a notary.

To hack an axe-haft
an axe
hacks;
the pattern 's near.

Let who weds never pass
too far
from his own class.

VI

Nine meshes of the net enclose
two sorts of fishes, bream, these, rudd, those:
Behold our Prince in his bright-broidered clothes.

Wild geese a-wing circle the isle;
The Duke's coming 's so short a while;

Wild geese seek land as but a pause in flight;
Return, and not to be here but a night;

The Dragon-Robe in so brief a stay,
Who'd neither cause us grief, nor stay away.

VII

Big bad wolf falls over his tail;
Dutiful Duke goes quiet along the trail
in his good red shoes so orderly?

Big bad wolf trips over his jowl,
let him fall on his tail and howl;
The Duke rings true.
Who'll carry thru?

HE.

PART

TWO

in eight books

ELEGANTIAE
or Smaller Odes

I

"Salt
lick!" deer on waste sing:
grass for the tasting, guests to feasting;
strike lute and blow
pipes to show how
feasts were in Chou,
                    drum up that basket-lid now.
"Salt
lick!" deer on waste sing:
sharp grass for tasting, guests to feasting.
In clear sincerity,
here is no snobbery.
This to show how
good wine should flow
                    in banquet mid true
                    gentlemen.
"Salt
lick!" deer on waste sing,
k'in plants for tasting, guests to feasting;
beat drum and strumm
lute and guitar,
lute and guitar to get
deep joy where wine is set
mid merry din
let the guest in, in, in, let the guest in.

II
REQUEST FOR FURLOUGH

Toiling stallions, winding road,
Would I were home, the king's load
is heavy as heart, on Chou Road,

Heavy team ever strains,
They be black with white manes;
would I were home, I am oppresst
by duty that gives a man no rest.

Doves can fly, then rest on oak
but the king's yoke heavy is
and my father in distress.

Weary pigeon can come to tree,
I cannot serve my mother fittingly.
There's no rest in
the king's livery.

By the black manes of my white horse
I yoke these words in remorse with this refrain:
Let me report to my mother again.

III
**Where the dunes come down from the lowland plain,
bright flowers, a legate's train
keen on their errand.**

163

Bright flower in lowland
that gallops
fearing to lose its hour,
the legate's train
astrain, each:

Horses like fillies,
reins drenched with sweat
from hard driving
for what news they can get;

Dapples on silky rein
push hard to catch as can
what the folk
of this land plan.

With six drenched reins
the whites with black manes
surge over all the plains
to measure reports;

Light grays with an even pull
urge, surge. Reports must be full.

FRATERNITAS

Splendour recurrent
in cherry-wood,
in all the world there is
nothing like brotherhood.

Brothers meet
in death and sorrow;
broken line, battle heat,
Brothers stand by;

In a pinch they collaborate
as the ling bird's vertebrae
when friends of either
protractedly just sigh.

Wrangle at home, unite outside
when friends of either are ready of course
to help either with anything
"short of brute force."

And peril past, there be those who
let brothers stew
in their own juice
as unfriends born, of no immediate use.

Set out the dishes
serve the wine,
let brothers dine tonight
with boyhood appetite.

Wife and childer together be
as sound of lutes played concurrently;
there's a deeper tone in fraternity
when elder and younger rise to agree.

Calm over earth, under sky
so be thy hearth and house as they should be;
probe to the utmost plan,
here the sincerity to rest a man.

"Takk! Takk!" axes smack
Birds sing "ying, ying"
From dank vale copse
to high tree tops
they fly and cry:
        a mate, mate, mate!

Shall we not seek cognate?
Spirits attend
him who seeketh a friend.
Air, hear our cry
concording harmony.

"Ugh! Ugh!" grunt woodmen all,
let the tree fall.
Wine strained, lamb fat, I call all
my dad's clan, if any come not, not
my fault, they were invited, all hereabout.
I've swept my court and washed it out,
for this meal:
eight courses and fatted veal.
None of my mother's folk have been slighted,
If they don't come they were, in any case, invited.

Hack tree on hill,
here's wine to fill
a whole line of cups and bowls;
When souls rot good food is wasted,
Sound wine 's here and to be tasted,
When it's gone we'll buy more.
Bang the pint-pot, foot dance, and dine,
use our leisure in circumstance!
Wine, wine, wine, WINE,
Wine after, and wine before.

VI
**The nobles reply to one of
the preceding "Deer Odes"**

Heaven conserve thy course in quietness,
Solid thy unity, thy weal endless
that all the crops increase and nothing lack
in any common house.

Heaven susteyne thy course in quietness
that thou be just in all, and reap
so, as it were at ease, that every day
seem festival.

Heaven susteyne thy course in quietness
To abound and rise as mountain hill and range
constant as rivers flow that all augment
steady th' increase in ever cyclic change.

Pure be the victuals of thy sacrifice
throughout the year as autumns move to springs,
above the fane to hear "ten thousand years"
spoke by the manes of foregone dukes and kings.

Spirits of air assign felicity:
thy folk be honest, in food and drink delight;
dark-haired the hundred tribes concord
in act born of thy true insight.

As moon constant in phase; as sun to rise;
as the south-hills nor crumble nor decline;
as pine and cypress evergreen the year
be thy continuing line.

VII

Pick a fern, pick a fern, ferns are high,
"Home," I'll say: home, the year's gone by,
no house, no roof, these huns on the hoof.
Work, work, work, that's how it runs,
We are here because of these huns.

Pick a fern, pick a fern, soft as they come,
I'll say "Home."
Hungry all of us, thirsty here,
no home news for nearly a year.

Pick a fern, pick a fern, if they scratch,
I'll say "Home," what's the catch?
I'll say "Go home," now October's come.
King wants us to give it all,
no rest, spring, summer, winter, fall,
Sorrow to us, sorrow to you.
We won't get out of here till we're through.

When it's cherry-time with you,
we'll see the captain's car go thru,
four big horses to pull that load.
That's what comes along our road,
What do you call three fights a month,
and won 'em all?

Four car-horses strong and tall
and the boss who can drive 'em all
as we slog along beside his car,
ivory bow-tips and shagreen case
to say nothing of what we face
sloggin' along in the Hien-yün war.

Willows were green when we set out,
it's blowin' an' snowin' as we go
down this road, muddy and slow,
hungry and thirsty and blue as doubt
(no one feels half of what we know).

VIII

We took out our carts to the fields beyond the wall.
Emperor's call. Told the teamsters to load.
The king's road is a hard road, a thorny road.

We took out our cars to the village beyond the walls,
our flags with the double snake and the ox-tails,
falcon and turtle flags flappin' about,
but the grooms are worn out.

Majesty ordered Nan Chung build the Fang wall;
we took out our cars lickety-clickety at the call,
plenty of flags with dragons and snakes —
Nan Chung give the Hien-yün the shakes
when he squared up the North Wall.

When we went out the grain was growin'
that 's on the mind now its drizzlin' and snowin',
sloggin' along in snow and mud,
king's work tough, however you look,
"Home?" we're afraid they'd chuck us the book.

Grasshoppers jumpin' chirruppy-churrp
"Not seen our men. Wish they'd come!"
That's what the women are sayin' at home.
Nan Chung 's a terror against the Jung.

Spring days gettin' long,
Now be the orioles in song,
Leaf-pickin' nearly done,
We pluckin' captives to learn what they know;
Goin' home, and the goin' is slow
But Nan Chung 's rolled out the rovin' hun.

IX

There's fine fruit on
the lone pear-tree
and no rest for the king's armee.
One day, then another day,
Sun and moon wearin' away,
October now, let a torn heart grieve,
Will they ever get their winter leave?

Lonely pear-tree full of leaves,
Government work, no reprieves,
Heart can break here in the shade,
Will they ever come back from that raid?

I climb the hill north of the town
to get in twigs of *k'i* willows
as the government work goes on.
Hard on the old folks;
"Broken car?"
"Horses foundered?"
"They can't be far."

They haven't even loaded yet,
Can't be coming; never get set.
He hasn't started, he'll never come.
My heart sadder than I can tell
I tried my luck by straws and shell,
They both said he was nearing home.

X

SOUTH TERRACE, no text.

One of the six "lost odes."

Title poem and four others lost, there being some discussion as to whether texts once existed, or whether the titles refer to the music only.

The "lost odes" have left their titles and numerals:

I. The white flower (of a blameless life).

II. The shu (panicled millet) flowers. A poem of the seasons.

IV. The keng sprouts. That keng being a very interesting ideogram, seventh of the ten stems, a path or orbit, the evening star, and to change or restore. Production in kind, cyclic, each in its time.

VI. The top of the pyramid, or mount veneration.

VIII. The sprouting of equity, how men came to observe it.

Banquet and dance songs, some of them probably sung by troops of dancers, others by guests and host.

III   170

Fine fish to net,
ray, skate;
Milord's wine is
heavy and wet.

Fish to trap,
bream, tench,
Milord has wine
to drink and quench.

Fine fish to trap,
carp and mud-fish,
Milor' has' wine
in quantities'h.

Food in plenty
say good food

Plenty of food
all of it good,

This the song each guest agrees on:
Milor's good food all fits the season.

V

(? ROUND IN CANON)

South lakes full of flickering fish,
Barbel make a pretty dish,
                    jab down that top-net on 'em!
A gent by liquor gets good guests,
                    blessings upon 'em!
Howk 'em up with a landing scoop,
He's got wine and a full troop,
                    blessings upon 'em!
Sweet gourds climb on southern trees;
Right 'uns are the sort that please
                    in gentleman's festivities.
Elegant doves,
good bottle-men,
Milord has wine,
Do come dine again.

VII

South Mount's shrub, North Mount's grass,
all the joy that ever was
in any state or family
is founded on gentility,
                    ten thousand years.
South Mount's berries, North Mount's willows
any state that gives light still owes
that lustre to its gentlemen
                    ten
                        thousand years.
South Mount's medlar, North Mount's plum,
a lord who keeps troth
is to his people both
                    father and mother,
                    fame without end.

South Mount's mangrove, North Mount's sloes
dark as nobles' aged brows,
age shall end not
joy of feasting
mid men of untarnished fame,

Vigour ever, South Mount's aspen
North Mount pine, wrinkled skin shall end not feasting,
loyal joy the hour outlasting
                    gentlemen to proof in testing
                    maintain and rule your after-line.

IX
THE SHINING DRAGON
(? of royal favour)

Thick southernwood
dew drenches,
the sight of Milord gives serenity,
on feasting benches
revelry;
lasting shall his praises be.

Thick southernwood
dew-soaked the night;
He's here all right
princely to sight;
tho' the dragon gleam
his eye stays straight
nor in old age
shall divagate
                    (unswerving honesty
                    not undermined in senility.)

Thick southernwood
dew-drenched the night;
he's here all right
dining fraternally.
When elder and younger brothers agree
age shall but strengthen their honesty.

Thick southernwood
dew-filled the night;
He's here all right.
To men of the gleaming rein
concord in every harness bell,
ten thousand lucks, and all's well.

Dew, deep lying,
Till day no drying,
Calm night outstaying
Let no dry man away.

Dew deep in grass
as manes pass,
calm thru night all
in clan hall
   feasting.

Dew on willow, dew on thorn;
as sun's head threadeth
each good knight treadeth,
of heart-sight, deed's born aright.

"Fellow-" and "trust-"tree fruit
nor think to do it;
true gentles so
do as they do.

(Gentle blood
breedeth rectitude.)

Deep, deep the dew
that will not dry till day;
Drink deep the night,
let none go dry away.

Deep, deep the dew
in the abundant grass;
Beneath this roof
ancestral manes pass.
Out-drink the night.*

* All of which ought to be got back into lyric form somehow.
 Grass receives dew, the courtiers an ethical or at least deportmental lead from their prince. The rest as in the first version.

92   II·2 THE WHITE FLOWER DECAD

BOOK 3. RED BOWS
Mainly songs of action, or dramatized dances recalling the hunts and campaigns? The red ceremonial bow conferred considerable authority on the recipient.

Unstrung red bow,
honour's token, honour'd guest,
from my heart's sincerity,
bang gong, bang drum
till the noon come,
                    feast.

Red bow unstrung
for honoured guest
to carry away
by my heart's cordiality
bang gong, bang drum
at my right hand
                    till the noon come.

Red bow unstrung,
case it, my guest.
By my heart's cordiality
bang gong, bang drum
till the noon come,
                    toast.

II

176

As in mid-mount, sandal tree,
His delight is in equity.

By the stream's marge stands a tree,
to have but seen him is jollity.

As asters grow in hills and dells,
I have seen him, and got five hundred cowrie shells.

Willow boat bobs to wave's cup or crest,
Now I have seen him, my heart is at rest.

When the sixth moon roosted, we got out the war-cars,
heavy equipment. Huns flamed raiding;
The king's command was: Peace in the kingdom.

Matched blacks in quadriga, trained and in order,
Ere that moon's end all was focus'd in our allotments,
So the king outed us to emperor's aid.

Great horses by fours, broad under fetlock
o'er-bore the hun dogs, doughty the duke's deed;
We stood to war's needs and order was in the kingdom.

Feckless huns town'd in Tsiao, seized Huo, lacking provisions,
scythed into Hao up to its border, unto King's north-bank.
Broidered our banners, bearing bird-signs,
bright white the pendants, ten ranks of war cars
van'd our advancing.

War-cars well-weighted; straight the stallions
trained to be trusty, struck at the Hien-yun;
drove to T'ai-Yüan; and Ki-fu
law'd all the states, in peace as in war time.

Ki-fu feasted then, much was afforded him.
From Hao homing our road ever long.
Wine to the worthy, minced carp and roast terrapin.
Chang Chung the filial is here.

Ready to reap the millet stands,
where was unused land ere Fang Shu took command.
3000 cars went to his wars.

Fang Shu's black-dappled team of four
drew his red-screened car to the war,
shagreen quiver and hooked breast-plate,
his rein-ends of metal ornate.

New grain for our supplies,
where was waste, hamlets rise
since Fang Shu took command of what had been fallow land
with 3000 lacquered cars, dragon flag and snake banneret,
bells in bridles and bit-ends set,
red knee-shields flash
and, at his girdle, pale green gems clash.

Swift flying hawk in heaven's gate
droppeth to stance and state, Fang Shu
to command
3000 cars
by band, manned, trained;
wheeled under flag, turned,
and, as the sun draws, Fang Shu:
to the deep of the drum, to forward and then
drew back the men
scattered in raiding.

Ghing crawlers chirrp'd at a great state,
Fang Shu was old but met their weight
(Ghing horde counted his age, and lost
went down in holocaust).
Chiefs brought for question here,
then with sound as of breaking thunder
with snorting
with flashing
his cars plowed the huns under.
The Ghing and Mann tribes knew fear.

As by the sun's force, promised, Fang Shu
crashed thru.

                        V

By fours the great stallions, pair'd as to prize
Drew our assault cars toward the sun-rise.

But good light field cars with the bull horses, pull thru
to the grassland and parkage near Fu.

Chief-huntsmen sound the halloo
as over burnt grass
beaters pass, each to place, and shake
signal flags, yak-tail, turtle-and-snake,
to take
game in Ao.

Atta horse, atta horse,
teams move as in chess,
gilt shoes, red knee-caps,
a hunt in court dress.

Thumb-ring and wrist-shield, bows bent in the same
instant, one volley heaps up the game.

Four bays, no swerve of the outer pair,
none out of step under the yoke,
howe'er they gallop each volley
hits as with one, I say ONE, axe-stroke.

Whinney in order, as the flags sign, they run;
beaters contend not, nor goes all the game to one great kitchen.

Who hunts so without clamour is a king
to avail in the great focussing.

                    VI   180

When the sun in his course
layed lance on the right mark of the dial
we bowed to the architype horse,
the senior, with rites of the season;
good hunting cars and good pullers
we went up the great dunes
to drive in the wild herds.

When the sun said it was cow day
we picked our ponies
and sought game in the plain,
antlered bucks, does. By the rivers of Shensi

                              was imperial hunting.
Game thick in that river land,
in covert or breaking it, grouped or turning
we charged right and left,
some herd 'em, some grapple
to make imperial banquet.

We bent our bows and aimed arrows,
let fly at young boars and big rhinos
so to serve guest and make meat for wine's wetting.
To every hunter and guest
at the evening meal shall come
the great horn
with wine of the best.

ALITER (and more briefly)

HILARE DIE, fifth in decade:
to the Ur-horse we prayed
with field-cars arrayed
bull horses tall chased the wild flocks
on high hill (malga) overall.

HILARE DIE, that of the seventh moon,
we picked our mounts to match game
(steeds swift as deer)
does and stags came thru
Ts'i and Tsü.
                An Emperor's ado.

Mid plain crowded, to start up or wait,
bevy and pair. We darted out left and right
to our Lord's delight.

Bent our bows till arrows reached arm-pit
Then shot down
young boar and stot,
rhino as well, to feast all guests
with sweet wine
fit to the test.

VII

Wild geese with a "whish" of wing,
officers go to the waste.
                "Toil, you lone fish."

From wing, geese nest in marsh,
we scholars raise a wall,
5000 toise in all to each day's stint
where quiet homes shall rise
from our toiled agonies.

Wild geese cry harsh a-wing
(wise see the toil)
Fools call us proud
and say:
                Too loud.

What hour is this? the court-yard flare burns bright,
we hear a chink of bit-bells thru the night.

We hear it faint: "chin-chink" across the night,
he comes not yet, the court-yard flare flicks bright.

What hour of dawn, the lanthorn wick smokes still
to greet his flag that crests yon eastward hill.

IX

CH'AO TSUNG *
Churning of water,
Homage to Thetis.

Churning waters pay court to Sea, in the East,
Swift-flying falcon cometh to rest
but who among you, brothers, countrymen, eldest or least
squarely faces this chaos,
                    having neither father nor mother?

Churning waters now overflowing all banks,
The hawk flies untamed and wild.
Bandits break ranks, there is no control,
They are not followed. Sorrow, not to assuage!

High hawk come to mid mount,
what the folk say is gone wrong
and no one opposes them. 'Ware friend, nor hold
their propaganda of no account. †

X

ON DECLINING OFFICE

The cranes cry over the nine marshes
and their cry sounds over the waste,
Fish go dark through the deep
or lie at rest by the isles,

Delight is in a garden of sandal-woods
with withered leaves blown beneath them,
Let some other hill's rock serve you for whetstone.

* The Tsung is the ancestral temple: pay court to, or come to the court.
† A mistranslation, but it may keep the student from coming to rest.

The crane cries over the nine pools of the marshland
and its sound carries up toward the sky,
fishes lie by isles or go seaward;

There is delight in the closed garden of sandal-woods,
grain now in the alleys between them:
Let some other hill's rock grind your jade.

BOOK 4. MINISTER OF WAR

I

"Lord of the Light's axe," * by what cause
should we, the king's teeth and claws
be cast into misery
'thout roof or stay?

Lord of the Light's axe, why should we officers
be cast into distress
that is
bottomless?

Minister of War, aye slow in the ear,
how hast construed
that a mother's corpse
is soldier's food.

II
SCALE ALTRUI

Garden sprouts for bright white colts,
tether and tie till mid-day,
nay, he's away
                    to ramble.

---

* The prayer ideogram composed of the two radicals: axe; and the light descending. Last character in the song explained in commentary as meaning that the old women would be worn out getting in kindling wood etc., work properly done by the filial sons. Commentary cites tradition that the Palace Guards were sent to the north frontier for defence after the disgraceful defeat of King Süan's regular forces there in 788 B.C.

Garden beans for these brilliant wee'uns,
tether and tie a welcome guest
                    for a good night's rest.

He could be duke or a marquis rather
would he foregather
with peers in our capital
                    but his delight
                    is to be eremite.

In deep vale to chew a spare bale
of scant hay, that a king's jewel were,
could he but bear
high life on another's stair.

III
HUANG NIAO

Yaller bird, let my corn alone,
Yaller bird, let my crawps alone,
These folks here won't let me eat,
I wanna go back whaar I can meet
the folks I used to know at home,
                    I got a home an' I wanna' git goin'.

Yalla' bird, let my trees alone,
Let them berries stay whaar they'z growin',
These folks here ain't got no sense,
can't tell 'em nawthin' without offence,
Yalla' bird, lemme, le'mme go home.
                    I gotta home an' I wanna' git goin'.

Yalla' bird, you stay outa dem oaks,
Yalla' bird, let them crawps alone,
I just can't live with these here folks,
                    I gotta home and I want to git goin'
                    To whaar my dad's folks still is a-growin'.

IV

I go the waste, weeds shade but to the knee;
Under thy roof alliance bade me come,
You do not feed me,
                    let me go home.

I walk the waste, these weeds my food;
I came invited, as I construed,
Let me go as I had come,
You do not feed me,
                    let me go home.

I walk the waste, with but rough weeds to taste;
off with the old kin, on with the new,
not for their riches,
                    yet change was due.

ALITER

I tread the waste, save bracken there's no shade,
I came your in-law
to an offered house, as you bade.

An ex-wife's no bond, you're wed anew,
to say she's rich, that were too much to say;
Just word: you see it now a different way.

V

189

By curvèd bank
in South Mount's innerest wood
clamped as the bamboo root, rugged as pine,
let no plots undermine
this brotherhood.

Heir'd to maintain the lines
carnal and uterine;
doors west and south,
reared up the mile-long house
wherein at rest to dwell,
converse and jest.

Tight bound the moulds wherein to ram down clay,
beaten the earth and lime gainst rain and rat,
no wind shall pierce to cold the Marquis' state
nor bird nest out of place,
here is he eaved,

who moves as on winged feet,
sleeves neat
as a pheasant's wing,
prompt as the arrow's point
to the bull's-eye.
And here the audience hall,

Rich court in peristyle
with columns high
their capitals contrived right cunningly;
cheery the main parts,
ample the recess
where he may have repose in quietness.

Mat over mat, bamboo on rush
so it be soft, to sleep, to wake in hush,
from dreams of bears and snakes?
                    Saith the diviner:
Which mean
Bears be for boys; snakes, girls.
Boys shall have beds, hold sceptres for their toys,
creep on red leather,
bellow when they would cry
in embroidered coats
ere come to Empery.

Small girls shall sleep on floor and play with tiles,
wear simple clothes and do no act amiss,
cook, brew and seemly speak,
conducing so the family's quietness.

VI

190

No sheep! Who says: No sheep?
300 to every flock.
Who says: No kine?
By nineties, of temple stock,
kink-horned the sheep, silk-ear'd the kine.

Some down to river-brink,
some drink pool'd streams;
to lie, to low.
Your hinds have thick leaf coats,
wide hats (bamboo), a-back their food-supplies.
Your beasts, by thirties, are ready for sacrifice.

Your herders rustle fagots, hens and cocks,
hemp-twigs to kindle fires; your flocks
'thout murrain, neck and neck,
sound mutton, solid,
rush to the pent-hold at the shepherd's beck,
such was their care.

The neat-herd dreams of fish, portending men;
of flags a-wind, turtle in toise, embannered falconry.
Many the fish?
Full shall the bushel be;
new homesteads rise
                after such augury.

VII

191

Abacus against high cloud, crag over crag, Mount South
to echo with cry on cry;
O'er-towering Yin, thou proud
as people cower, burning with inner heat
daring no open jest, so soon an end,
the hour all-seen, save in thy mind.

Grade over grade, Mount South,
so thick thy gnarl of wood,
Lord Yin, thou proud,
unjust in tyranny, the corners of heaven reek death,
no man to praise thy chaos in disease,
you cast no fault aside.

Yin, viceroy
"foundation stone" of Chou
to judge and bind state's weal
as on a potter's wheel
the Emperor's "Next" defined
by title but not by fact,
Unmuddle the mass,
Make it possible for folk to be honest.
Fell glare of sky, pitiless
caving our troops to but a hollow shell,
this is unright.

Without presence, without affection:
among the people no faith, no word-keeping.
No enquiry, no appointments (no delegation of power).
With proper levels, proper dismissals
there would be no ambiguous minor officials,
nor your picayune in-laws in fat government jobs.

Heaven in dither
wrangles rain hither.
Glare sun's unkindness
sendeth great (moral) blindness.
When gentles attain,
people regain
quiet; be gentles just,
hates must
go out.

Dire sun over sky, no polar force;
no parts hold to calm course; *
'tis as if moon's fiat
wrought folk's unquiet.
Heart stupefied
drunk with grief, who 's to guide
the state straight, who hold plow-handle. †
If king rule
not himself, to all clans 'tis dule,
Four steeds take yoke
stretch necks to the four coigns and see
in every coign, misery.

Prodded of hate
lancing today who is
next day's cup-mate.

O Heaven un-level, this king unstill,
mending never a fault, hateth all ordered will.

Kia-Fu has raised this verse
to probe the King's evil mood;
let him work his heart to this form
and a thousand towns can have food.

* New crops of woe each month.
† Quis clavum afferat?

Frost's nimble silk
beneath a summer moon
cuts heart, men's talk the more.
Double-talk on the up,
I am alone,
My heart, ai! ai!
gnawed to the bone.

2

Begat me, you twain, to pain
in the mid cult of mouth-talk,
nor before, nor yet shall be
that grief, the more it's real,
draws more insult.

3

In doleful dumps, having no salary,
vacant in thought, this thought comes over me:
other non-criminals may soon be vexed
— hack-driving — to find paid jobs,
nor know where crow lights next.

4

Mid-wood now scrub and bare deforested,
mere fagot-twigs where once the tall trees stood;
the heaven 's in nightmare, yet it once was able
to run smooth course, to all men merciable,
none to withstand it. And it hates what man?

5

Call mountain mole-hill, the high crest says: you lie.
Double-talk runs, not even in jeopardy.
Call the diviners, and their vapid blocks
emit: We're wise, who knows crow-hens from -cocks?

6

"The heaven's lid high," not dare to stand up straight;
"The earth's crust thick," not dare to not tread light;
and mark these words that have both order and spine,
while you chameleons turn more serpentine:

7

Thick wheat mid rocks upon the terraced hill,
The sky-shake knocks, as tho' it could not fix me,
seeking my style, and yet cannot annex me,
hating at length
yet using not my strength.

8

Sorrow at heart, as tho' by cords constricted;
grind of his reign whereby are all afflicted
to quench that lamp whereby wide earth was lit,
Proud hall of Chou.
                  Pao Sy 'll abolish it.

9

Thought's tread at end beneath the cold of rain,
knock off the cart-props till the load fall out,
and then cry: Lord, is there no help about?

10

not slip the cart poles, that be true spokes-men?
Keep eye on driver in perils, and you won't overturn
but reach hard track's end.
                  That's not your concern.

11

A shallow basin gives the fish no shade,
dive as they will, there's flash of fin's knife-blade;
Sorrow in heart for any shred or flaw
to see the state, and all, neath tiger's claw.

12

Good wine, good victuals;
neighbours, come to dine,
praise from feeding kin.
I've but my skin
alone, to keep grief in.

13

The low have houses and the mean get tips,
Folk with no salary
the heavens swat,
While ploots can manage
and the "outs" cannot.

IX
Of Queen Pao Sy,
Huang's town planning at Hiang,
and the Solar Eclipse
of 29 August 776 B.C.

The sun was eaten
when the green moon-sprout
saw August out,
Sin-Mao, the day
(sky's acrid 8, earth's 4)
Ugly, and how.
Moon gnawed out, sun under yoke,
Pity the folk
                    beneath.

2

Sun, moon, foretell
evil? run wild,
State without rule,
good men exiled.
Moon's gnawed out in normal course,
What imprecise force
swallows the sun?

3

Flame-flower flasheth
with dire lashing
of cloud's tail in all-quake;
no covered quiet,
no sky's seal.
The 100 rivers o'erflow,
mountains are fallen,
high crests become valleys,
vale reared into summit,
and as for man now:
none changeth a fault.

4

Not Huang-fu the Premier,
nor Fan at the Cultura Popolare,
nor Kia-Po of the Interior,

nor Chung-yün of Logistics,
nor Tsou the recorder,
nor Kuei at the War Office,
nor Kü of the Heavies;
But she?
　　　　　flames away, dwelling in splendour.

5

Will Huang-fu say:
　　　　　　　Not the moment?
Does he stir us without representation;
to shift our roofs and our house-walls?
Plow-land to bent and waste moor,
mid which vexations he says:
　　　　　"I am not tyrannous,
　　　　　These are the regulations."

6

Our prudent Huang has had a building scheme
and three contracting lords are now enriched,
There 's no police chief left for royal guard,
the hunting set has been, all, led Hiang-ward.
(To Huang's new town, that is.)

7

I dare not post a monthly works report,
knowing the mare's-nest it would raise in court.
It is not heaven has sent these torments down,
this devil's brew boils from the talk of town.*

8

Far, far my village
in cark of care,
there 's a state surplus, I alone
worry, everyone else resigns.
Sole not to rest, impenetrable
word of the sky
that says not why I presume
not to copy these friends of mine:
Resign!
　　　　　Damn'd if I will, I were as ego'd as they.

* Gush of conversation, back biting and interoffice contentions come UP out of men.

Light, light aloft   slow in thy deed,
crystal thy flow   deadly our need,
swifter to earth   death, famine, dearth;
lopped off the state. Autumnal sky
awful thy might,   feckless, unplanned:
One eddying punishment
sinks guilty and innocent.

                    2

Chou's breed washed out,   nowt to hitch to,
The big shots quit,   there's none to know
if I do my bit; how I sweat.
The three top men cut short their office hours,
fief courts don't sit to hour or date,
All talk duty   and turn to hate.

                    3

Light over sky   if princes lie
what hath man to steer thereby?
An hundred lords respect themselves? Not even!
By that the less revere each other, or heaven.

                    4

From war learned nothing, nor from famine either,
two plagues to warn him and he learned from neither.
Will you hear truth from a poor worn-out groom
when coward princelings fear to use the broom,
nor dare speak truth when asked for their advice,
but at the least whisper vanish in a trice?

                    5

Ill 's beyond speech. Speak truth and suffer for it,
Fat jobs to those who, with flow of words, ignore it.

                    6

Accept an office? That is thorns and death,
that to refuse will be lèse-Emperor;
to take? a peril that even your friends incur.

7

And if I say to you: come back to court.
"No town house, I've no house," is your retort.
For tears and blood, and every word incur
hate. When you went out
Who followed as carpenter.

BOOK 5. LESSER COMPLEYNTS

I
"PLANNERS" RAW DEAL
770 B.C. approx.

Heaven's worry, scurries to earth;
twisty planning, what's to block it?
At sight of good plan, they turn to rotten again,
the sight of their planning
gives me a pain.

2

First say yes, then say no; *
good plan, no go,
but a rotten they dress in flummery,
the sight of their planning worries me.

3

Tired turtles, clean petered out
decline to bother with human doubt
(poked hot sticks into tortoise shells †
which answer us no oracles)
planners and planners pullulate
concluding nothing (not even debate).
Worders are it
in the king's abode,
no one dares put his name on a chit;
all maps and no marching
                              covers no road.

* Aliter:
        Dirty water and slanders run
            together in yes-men and drain pits.
† Answer given by the way the shell splits from the heat.

4

Our active designers
don't like old ways —
irked by the solid symmetrical —
but let 'em hear the sound of a phrase,
they'll quarrel over it days and days
as builders who change for the last thing told 'em
never get a house to hold 'em.

5

State
all a wobble,
scanners and boobs —
a few left to gobble —
bright boys and planners,
some who'll "take trouble"
all of a bubble
down into quick-sand.

6

No tool 'gainst tiger,
no boat for river,
That much, no more,
and they know it;
but above all to be precise
at the gulf's edge
or on thin ice.

II
GNOMIC VERSES

196

Ring-dove, my gentle, to sing and fly
Wingèd to circle, up and away
I think of antiquity, men of old gone,
And of those two, at wake of day.

2

The wise drink and hold their wine, but topers say
that to be drunk is to be rich for a day.
Yield men, all men, this advice:
Heaven speaks once and never twice.

3

Beans mid plain, plain folk pluck 'em,
Bug had a boy but the mud-wasp took him;
Better be careful to train your sons
to be clean, as your pattern runs.

4

Collaboration will never fail
between the two ends of the bright wag-tail,
first to sing and then to fly
as the days and the moons pass by
a slug-a-bed shames his family.

5

Orioles flicker across the sky
and then pick grain from the threshing floor,
We get jailed if we pick up more;
good and evil run nip and tuck
so I'll scatter this grain to try my luck.*
(responsus est?)

6

Man ought to sit quiet as bird on bough,
cagey as edging a precipice,
light-foot as treading on thin ice.

Capped crows flap in flock
home. I am alone to weather shock;
For what evil done to the sky
hath my heart misery?

2

Chou road that level was,
now hidden under wild grass,
heart-ache, unsleeping a-bed,
old before time, grieved body and head.

---

* Some form of divination answered by noting how the birds pick up the scattered grain, or rice.

3

Mulberries and catalpas of farm-stead be to revere,
Father and mother more dear;
am I not carnal and uterine?
What birth-hour ill-chosen as mine?

4

Thick are the willows, the broad locust thin of voice,
cool are the reeds about the dark-deep pool,
I, like a boat a-drift, come to no rest;
sleep not for worry burrowing in my breast.

5

So easy a-foot in wild-wood the stags run,
Pheasant aloft seeks mate as moon fades from the sun,
I, like a sickened tree losing its boughs,
with ache at heart now dark as no man knows.

6

Men shelter the hunted hare,
bury the corpse by wayside,
but the prince (my father) has gripped his heart.
Tears, tears, never dried!

7

As if sworn on the wine cup
he gives credence to lies he has not examined,
compassionless. But men fell trees by their lean,
where they be thick; split fagots by grain.
He shelters the guilty,
Mine is the pain.

8

Naught stands higher than mount,
nor is hollow deeper than water-fount;
that the Prince have not light nor dark in his words —
ears be in echoing wall,
Let him keep from my weir and fish-trap who hath
neither examined my case
nor the aftermath.

Sky, my father, I have not sinned,
I am confused,
Terrible mother aloft,
I have not sinned,
Glare light,
            it is not my guilt.

2

Chaos in sperm
usurped submergedly
soaking in, secretly;
burst to twice life when Milord
believed calumny.
Would he show preference,
Joy, rage,
crooks would hence; it would all stop,
and speedily.

3

Multiple treaties drag confusion out,
belief in thieves adds violence to doubt,
Bandits' sweet talk but more enflames the blaze,
mid which incoherence
'twill be the King who pays.

4

A superior man
raised the great bric-a-brac,
the temple's apse and fore;
great plan needeth great architect.
I can but track
plain man, plain crook, hot-foot in plain affair
as hounds run a sly hare,
my similar.

5

Gentlemen, as I've heard tell
plant trees that are workable; *
many minds among wayfarers, mind 'ee,

* "Il n'y a rien de plus désagréable que l'acajou." — French cabinet-maker in 1924.

on the high road North and South
twisty tall talk comes from the mouth
and words soft as the shamisan
distinguish the thick-faced man.

6

Which kind teeters here on the stream's brink,
no fist, no force, making mess
in already muddled offices?
Swollen legs give 'em acumen?
Planning lots of things they'll do when,
they get what they haven't, namely: men.

V

What sort of chap —
twisty mind — 's come
to my dam, not to my door?
What now and how?
Ganged up with Pao.

2

There were two in this devilment,
to pass in silence evil meant and
There was a different tale to tell
before you found me "impossible."

3

What can he be, on my garden path
unseen, but heard talking as they went by,
no shame before men, no awe of sky.

4

Neither North nor South, can't blow straight,
but as whirl-wind
come to my dam to disturb my mind.

5

Travelling easy, that's the rub
and no time to come in. Hurried you'd stop to grease hub
and wheel, and you haven't called once
to see how I feel.

6

Would be pleased to see you and du'nno why
you take this notion of passin' me by,
never once in to ease the eye.

7

Old duets with flute and pipe,
we used to play 'em stripe by stripe;
Believe you don't know me? Dog, pig and cock
mark my oath on the chopping-block.

8

If you were a devil or water-sprite
one couldn't see you by daylight,
but looking you eye to eye
one can see all that there is to see
and get, in out and out prosody,
eh? a near-total silhouette.

VI

200

Such elegant streaky lines in brocade
till the solid shell is made;
liars by littles ply their trade.

2

Stitch a-sky, dot, the South Sieve's made.
Who loves to aid
these smearers in the smearing trade?

3

Winging,
gad about,
tittling, tattling
to be found out.

4

The quickness of the hand deceives the eye
and repetition suaves mendacity,
Non obstat, you'll be ousted bye and bye.

5

Proud men ride high to watch the workers sweat,
O'er-hanging heaven look down upon their pride
and pity those on whom the yoke is set.

6

Take therefore, I say, these smearers
and fellow travellers, chuck 'em
to wolves and tigers, and if the striped cats spew 'em forth,
offer 'em to the Furthest North.
If the old pole decline to spare 'em place,
kick 'em clean off it into stellar space.

7

And here's my address, I am still
at Willow Hollow Road by Acre Hill,
Meng Tsy has lost his balls but makes this verse,
let the administration heed it, or hear worse.

VII
EAST WIND   201

Soft wind of the vale
that brings the turning rain,
            peril, foreboding;
Come time of quiet and revelry
you'll cast me from your company.

2

Idle the valley wind, hot tempest then,
far in your pleasure, near in your pain.
Came time of quiet revelry
You cast me from your company.

3

Scorching breath on the height, grief,
all grass must die, no tree but loseth leaf
Soft is the valley wind, harsh on the crest,
You remember the worst of me
Forgetting the best.

Waving ling? not ling but weed,
You two begat me, by labour to need.

Weed or plant that gives no grain,
you two begat me in toil and pain.

Shamed the jug that fills no cup;
orphan's life, proverb saith,
is worth less than early death.
Who sustaineth the fatherless?
Who stayeth the motherless?
Carry gagged grief beyond the court-yard wall,
In my house there is no one at all.

You who begat me, you who bore,
suckled and fed me long from your store,
embraced me at parting and when I came in,
by my candour I would have made return,
my luck runs ill, having no end nor bourne.

Harsh over South Mount
the whirl-winds moan,
all men have grain, I suffer alone.

Plod, plod, South Mount,
wind blows unceasingly,
I am the only grainless man
who does not die.

IX

Of the old barbecues and a new
plutocracy, adorned but useless
as the constellations. Ascribed
to time of King Liu.   203

Heaped grain-platters, long thorn-wood spoon,
Chou road smooth as a whetstone
arrow-shaft-straight,
Gentles walking it, small folk, sedate, observe.
Looking back on this, it appears
in the mind. Define it? Save by my tears?

2

In small states of the East, and in great
no loom clicketh.
Shuttles are still, rollers turn not, the frost pricketh
thru the thin fibre of espadrilles.
Spindly duke's sons on Chou road now,
What hath been here, to and fro,
                    to outlast it?
                    The mind's sorrow.

3

Let not the flow of this chill melancholy
rot the cut wood;
tax on tax, tally on tally,
I wake and sigh for our poor folk,
small cut wood to pile and carry,
then can they rest from cart and yoke?

4

Down east the boys can't draw their service pay,
while western youth's a luxury display,
Where boatmen's sons are sporting bear-skin coats
the farm-boy bureaucrat tries, fails, and gloats.

5–6

Some will for wine who won't for broth
and wear great belt-gems, whose worth 's but froth.
A river of stars is lit across the heaven,
Trine Damsels * weave to the seventh house at even
with seven ply
for us nor cloth nor sign.
That eye-full of led oxen in the sky
draws not our farm carts here terrestrially.
Dawn's in the East, in West, Hyads nestle at ease.
East Venus, West Hesperus
to open and date the day,
Sky hath a rabbit-net that takes
                    naught save its way.

* Vega and the other two stars of the triangle.

7

South hath a Sieve that sifts us out no grain,
The northern Ladle dips us up no wine.
As the unsieving sieve might give tongue to attest
The handle of the Ladle is in the west.

X

June 's mid-summer, August brings coolth again;
The ancestral spirits are harsh, were they not men?

2

Autumn sees the plants wither,
wild beauties decline together;
all things cold now as pain,
I turn to go home again.

3

Winter day sparkles with snow, turning winds moan,
Others have luck, all of them. I am alone.

4

There be fine growths a-mountain,
Lord of the Chestnut, Marquis Plum
by ruin of roof-tree come
to banditry, and none to guess
their curdle of bitterness.

5

Spring water floweth, both to clear and in mud,
my days are but built up calamity; how call this good?

6

Floods of the Kiang and Han,
churning, South States record.
Worn out with service
I get no reward.

7

The quail and kite take air,
sturgeon hath lair
in deep waters evading.

8

Bracken hath crest,
Willow its rest in marsh
taking no wrong,
        my rest:
        a song.

BOOK 6. NORTH MOUNT

I

Officer and gentleman
sent to pluck medlars   on Mount Po Shan
all day, all day never to swerve
from the king's work, and my parents to serve
in grief.

2

Under the scattered sky all lands are fief,
all men to the sea's marge serve but one chief
and there is no justice known to the great,
I go alone   but straight.

3

Four stallions, bang, bang, hither and yon,
isn't it fine that I'm "not old"
and so few ready to do what I'm told
and my back still strong and straight
enough   for a border state.

4

That some men loll in banquet bout
and others work till clean worn out;
Some for the state in bed to lie,
others on road incessantly.

5

Some root mid ladies in luxury,
all in the king's cause naturally
and never hear a harsh command,

the rest of us sweating distractedly
in heavy harness incessantly
(from head to tail)
with both a pack and the martingale.

6

Some wine deep in rich luxury,
others be torn by anxiety;
fear blame, driven in, driven out
as the winds jerk,
year long, year long, nothing but work.

II

Let the Great Cart alone,
'ware dust.
Think not on sorrows
lest thy heart rust.

Push no great cart
lest dust enflame thine eye,
brood not on sorrows
lest joy pass by.

Push not the great wheel-spoke in moil and sweat
lest thou make thy troubles
                              heavier yet.

III

Light upon light that shines above the sky,
naught here on earth evades thy glittering eye;
We, who invade the West and pass
the steppe of K'iu over wild grass,
set out beneath a February moon
going thru cold and heat.
Now bitter poison rankles in the mind
thinking of courts and ease
we weep and would go home —
fearing the penalties.

2

Long, long ago we set out
thinking the sun and moon veering about
would see us home at the year's turn,
heavy in mood to brood that I alone
work for that crowd —
no furlough allowed,
longing for home,
fearing the price.

3

Sun and moon in their ingle
when we set out, now we'd about
in longing for home, work here piled on
more miserable
now's the year's end, to get harvest in,
of that harvest I pick not a bean
nor get southernwood;
think of their ease in offices
and go as far as the first night's inn,
lose nerve:
                    "be sent back again."

4

Haro! ye gentles, think 'ee that ease endures
and that no quake shall shake your sinecures?
Best take an honest colleague now and then
to attract the favouring spirits of the air
and keep the official process in repair.

5

Ergo, milordlings, loaf not too much
but look upon your jobs as really such,
Show sometimes liking for clean government
that the airy powers concede your preferment.

IV

Cl-ang, cl-ang go the bells,
turgid the Huai, clashing of waters
till sorrow has torn the mind
and the lords of old time go not out of heart.

2

Gong over gong, cold waters driven
till the heart is riven for the clear deeds
of the lords of old
                flawless.

3

Bells, drums, over the three isles of Huai
till the heart is moved that we see not their like
                who were here before us.

4

"*Ch-in, ch-in*" of the bells,
two lutes, organ and stone
in even tone,
so shall the "Elegantiae,"
so shall the "South" be sung,
                nor flutes shall mar.

V

209

They have cleared the thorn from this place
how, here, in the old days? Here was grain sown in the old days
abundant, here was grain
for the rites, for the barns,
for distilling
that we offer up with corn and wine to the spirits
that they aid us aye and the more.

2

Here move we quiet in order
here be led cattle spotless and rams
for the rites of winter and autumn,
flayers, boilers and carvers
and they who lay out and make ready
to invoke the spirit of banners,
to invoke the spirit of light,
to the spirits outspaced like banners,
to the glory of brightness,
to the source of the dynasty
here in his cartouche
white-shining, our sovran.

May the spirits aid in the banquet,
may the filial line never fail,
all this in the aim of plenty
10,000 years and with no bound.

3

That they be alert at the pyres and ovens of barbecue
slow moving near the tall stands
for the baked meats and the grilled meats,
that they care for small trays,
no flaw, tho' they be many;
that the guests take the communion cup in due turn
each back to each, thus reciprocal
a rite for the observance of equity
that there be ease and good confidence
the word spoken smiling;
that the sustainers, spirits, also come in due order
that the end be abundance,
good vintage, 10,000 years.

4

We have gone thru with the fire rite
and no fault, the flamen has made the announcement,
he conveys this to the heir
       at the second stance by the altar,
the fumes of the filial incense are perfume,
the souls in the air lust after your drink and victuals,
your luck is an hundred fold.
As is the hidden so is the pattern,
as the service was orderly
there shall be early harvest.
There has been order,
there has been promptness
(we have beaten the ground for the grain spirit.)
You have brought basket-offering and in order
there shall be yield to the maximum
       thru time without end.

5

The service of the equities has been carried out in detail
gong and drum have alerted,
the heir sits to receive the augur's announcement

the airy spirits (the spirits who go upward)
have all drunk and stand upright (cease drinking)
The representative of the White Splendour (the halo'd)
has risen
drum and gong sound: (nunc dimittis)
the spirits, sustainers, have instantly ascended back to their dwelling.
All the servants and noble dames
clear away with celerity,
the men of the patronymic
repair to their private feast.*

6

Enter musicians playing adagio
quieting music for favours to follow.
Your victuals are served,
no one grumbles, all is congratulation (or jollity),
they have drunk and eaten their fill,
the airy souls lust for your drink and victuals,
may they give you years and old age,
very benevolent, very timely
and in totality, sons' sons and grandsons
that they go not out of lordship in leading.

VI
YÜ'S CONTOUR FARMING, BONIFICA   210

Aye by South Mount Yü began
tilling for man
by dyke and drain
squared plain land and low.
His sons' sons' sons', have it so now
bound and townland south and east.

2

The heaven above stands as one arch of cloud,
falls snow, fine sleet
plus drizzle and soak
riching, by mulch, full favour the grain
of all our folk.

* Karlgren admirably, "lay feast"; purely human, not haunted.

3

Field by field as feather by feather
with ditch and dykes
sleek millet spikes (shu and tsi)
high harvested
give the heir wine and bread,
aye, to ten thousand years
to honour the manes of his ancestors,
   they as guests to his offering,
   he in ripe age.

4

Huts in mid field and melons by the banks,
candy their pulp also for offering
to his line's source, our thanks
and this shall bring sky's grace in age.

5

Clear wine in sacrifice to heaven's light
an healthy bull, red, to the great tablet's lord
with tinkle of bells at the knife's hilt
parting the hair, fat and blood spilt.

6

An holy reek to rich the temple air
in honour of Brightness
and to ten thousand years, invoke
our halo'd sires: exchange
luck for this smoke,
unbroke by time.

VII

Fair fields outspread yield an hundred
measures for one.
High grain a-field, hundred-fold yield.
Old crop meets new. Our farmers here
be fed all the year,
aye, from of old, such yield hath been.
So shall we go to south lots now
to weed and hoe
millet enow (shu and tsi) shall abundant be
to aid and set homestead
for the best cadets we've bred.

2

By the brightness of the altar vessels arranged;
by the pureness of the victim ram;
by the power of Earth and the square
bean fields generous, and tillers prosperous
to strum lute, archilute; beat drum;
come processional * to meet the Lord of the Field,
so pray we rain be sweet
that millets twain (tsi and shu)
grain our yeomen
and women.

3

Antient of line, here now's the Heir.
Wives, weeuns, bear
lunch baskets out.
The inspector 's about
south fields now to see what's good
and dips his hand
in everyone's food,
left, right, he says, to taste
what is dainty and what waste.
Grain even high o'er all we scan.
Calm lord maketh a ready man.

4

Heir mid his crop,
Grain flows over the reapers' scythes
as water over dam's top, or as thatch
to stack like humpy islands in the field.
A thousand barnes be filled,
10,000 carts,
millet, rice, maize, reapers have taken
be thus 10,000 years' prosperity,
and unshaken.

VIII

212

Great plowlands need
many chores, seed,
tools and forecare.

* ?Corpus Domini: "La procession va à travers les champs."

Grind share and go
start with the plow on south slopes now.
Let the grain grow
then pile it high in courtyard where
As grandsire was, is now heir.

2

Come sprout, come ear,
hard grain and good
let every weed and tare,
gnaw-bug and worm,
caterpillar, slug
fall dead in flame,
honour to T'ien Tsu,
in fact and name,
                                    God of the field.

3

Thickens the cloudy sky
that rain like a slanting axe
feed our Duke's field
then bless our yield,
We reap not miserly,
old women and poor follow our spoor.
To their relief
leave loosened sheaf,
short stock and unripe ear.

4

Now's come Greatgrandsire's heir,
women and youngsters bring
lunches to the men labouring
on the south slope, the overseer
does reverence to the four Corners of Air;
pours back the wine to earth (that gave the wine)
red bullock and black
pay for the millet crop;
by offer and sacrifice
funnel us further felicities.

Waters of Lo swirling and bound,
our prince has found true measure
(that is, the norm, his rest,
plenty with regularity,
as reed or thatch)
As red leather covers the knee
so stand six army corps
neat in their panoply.

2

Glinting Lo with never a drought,
as sword fills the jewelled scabbard's mouth,
so is he fit to last ten thousand years
and pillar up his house.

3

Waters of Lo, never a break in your flow
or his equity; that he bring
10,000 years
to all his clans prosperity.

The year puts on her shining robe
of flowers and leaves in broidery
amid the flower of viscounts court-dressed
I can give praise to quietness.

The year puts on his shining robe
that is rue's yellowest pageantry
The flower of viscounts in orderliness
be as chapter and verse of happiness.

The year puts on her shining robe
of yellow flowers and flowers white,
so comes each lord holding six smooth reins;
his four white horses have jet black manes.

Left goes left where it should be,
right goes to right accordingly,
I therefore praise these gentlemen
who know and show both the how and when.*

BOOK 7. SANG HU
The Haw Finch, or bird rather like
an oriole that arrives when the
mulberry comes into leaf.

I
"Bright clothes hide not true virtue."
A king greets his princes   215

Criss-cross on flaming wing
may these orioles get full blessing;
and gentles who sing.

Criss-cross gleaming throat,
by orioles I mean
gentlemen who are
the whole state's screen,

A flying buttress, wings of the laws,
model to show how things be done;
to them happiness rightly won,

neither in rashness,
neither fearful of hardness,
neither boastful in the day of good fortune.

To them sound wine and gentle thought
when the great ivory horn is brought
each unto each in proper turn to all,
this luck, long, long to abide —
into pit of pride
ne'er may we fall.

* A prince welcomes or replies to the feudatories who may have spoken the foregoing
in fact or in pantomime.

II

The Nobles reply to the foregoing
"Kün tsy wan nien"
That the gentleman last 10,000 years
216

Big duck fly yellow over hand nets and wide nets spread even
"Kün tsy wan nien"
May his happiness flow in harmony with earth and with heaven.

2

Big duck stand on the dam, and stretch left wings * in amity
"Kün tsy wan nien"
May we have, in leisure, felicity.

3

Teams in his stable, stall feed and war grain
"Kün tsy wan nien"
May his wealth be doubled again.

4

Steeds in his stable, war grain and stall feed
"Kün tsy wan nien"
That he have, ever, abundance over his need.

III
217

Leather caps, sound wine, good food,
where all be kin,
Here is no outer man,
all be of our father's clan
as mistletoe to cypress tree
to their chief in fealty —
worried without him, glad he's here.

Caps of leather, sound wine, good food in season,
Where else? how else? for what reason
could such a company foregather?
As mistletoe to pine
close knit to clan and line,
no stranger here has part,
and from thy face
the movements of my heart.

* Left wings: Legge says ducks head to tail. Similar defence manoeuvre of bulls in ring,
able to watch approach of attack from either direction.

Leather on head, food good, wine sound,
gathered round, so many a-kin;
melting flakes fall ere hard snow sets in,
sorrow and death attend no man's desire.
Slake well thy thirst before the even come
while ye have brothers' eyes to see
and ere ye tire.
Princely is leisure,
no man drinks here for hire.

IV

Hot axle, I drove, drove
to my love
             hasting,
neither food nor drink
             tasting.
I thought of her inwit,
No friends with me
             feasting.
Pheasant finds home
in flat forest,
My heart a nest
in her thought
             resting.

218

In with the lynch-pin, thought to a lady,
the youngest, the charmer, and go,
not by thirst, not for hunger,
the clear tone of her mind attests:
perfect feast needs no great guests.

2

In level forest pheasant makes nest
a level head to lesson me
how a model feast is laid
that long love unwearied be.

3

Our wine but vin ordinaire,
we share spare
food but with jollity
and my inferior character
will serve to sing and dance with her.

4

On ridge my stroke
lops bough from oak
fagots for fire wood
mid the thick underbrush where was leaves riot
if so thou come to eye
my heart hath quiet.

5

This I foresaw a-drive
when I went forth to wive, urging my horses
over mount, over hill, my six reins as lute-strings tight,
I drove aright
under Hesper, thee to meet,
so is my heart made suave with the heat.

V   219

Flies, blue flies on a fence rail,
should a prince swallow lies wholesale?

Flies, blue flies on a jujube tree,
slander brings states to misery.

Flies, blue flies on a hazel bough
even we two in slanderers' row
                        B'zz, b'zz, hear them now.

VI   220

Guests at mat in due order
left, right, big dish in centre,
sauces at border;
wine suave and sun'd as wine should be,
out of wine cometh unity,
                        bang the drum and strike the bell

After toast comes archery
all in due formality:
                "Show your bow-skill!"
                "'t's a hit if I do."
                "The cup with three legs goes to you."

2

With six-holed flutes
that were bamboo shoots,
drum time, with pantomime
to our line's root:
            Noel! Noel! that fiery rite delight
            HIM, the flame, our light
in flow, in rite
till the hundred rites all
be done here in hall
to phallus' and forest's purity
that thy line enduring be
deep as all continuity;
so deep the lust
each man here must
            laud thy coherence.
         Rivals grasp hands, ere hence
         comes One from ingle:
            "Let no man drink single,
            but dip and pour
            great cup's honour
                welding thy seasons."

3

Guests start eatin', mild and even,
The sober sit an' keep behavin',
but say they've booz'd then they do not.
When they've booz'd they start a-wavin' an' a-ravin',
Yas' sir they rise up from the ground
and start dancin' an' staggerin' round
each to his own wild fairy fancy
as they never would when sober.
Sobers sit and drunks go gay
elegant or with display
in order or in indecency.
         Drunks never know sufficiency.

4

When they've drunk they'll stagger and yell
and upset their plates as well,
dancing like devil masks from hell,
don't know the post house (where to stop)

with their crooked caps a-top
they canna' dance, but stagger and flop.
They'd be welcome to their pleasure
if they'd go when wholly soused
but to be booz'd and not to go
we define as lèse virtù
(failure, that is, to correlate
outward act with mental state)
But drinkin' 's great
up to proper measure.

5

And as at every drinking bout
some can hold it and some pass out,
we appoint, at every rally,
a toast-master and his keep-tally
so that those who can't hold their liquor
or, as we say, run true to form,
are kept from worse enormity
of word or of activity;
after three cups cannot tell lamb
from hornèd ram, but still
want more liquor ardently.

VII

THE CAPITAL IN HAO

Not to stir trouble from down up,
or vice-versa.

221

Fine fish in weed, that is their place.
And the king's good wine in his palace.

Fish in pond-weed wagging a tail
And the king in high Hao at his wassail.

While fish in pond-weed lie at ease
the kings of Hao may live as they please.

VIII

The fountain of honour is not
the fountain of produce.

222

Princes coming to court the king
and I've nowt to give for the beans they bring,

be the baskets round or square
as they come with car and four.
A black or an ax-coat * to wear?

2

Mid hornéd bubbles at the spring's threshold
as the leaves of cress † unfold
nobles come, their flags a-flap
jangle of bells at bridle strap
of trace horse or pole horse in harness,
princes coming to pluck the cress.

3

Red leather (aprons) above the knees
and, below them, side-cut puttees,
and with cordial alacrities;
Sky's Son's command
can renew rents and titles to land.

4

Oak's thick-leaved boughs,
Welcome, welcome!
that shade this house
welcome!
ten thousand lucks alight
on ye, to left and right,
cohort and liegemen,
rear guard and flank
    Justice and order
    guard the Imperial House.

5

Willow boat by a mooring rope,
Welcome, Lords, to these assizes
in the hope of richer prizes,
easier rents that ever more
ye may lie snug as dog neath door.

* Insignia of rank.
† Take cress, i.e. examination with prizes.

IX

GNOMIC VERSES

Snow that is watery dust

> Strong is the horn-tipped bow,
> bend it again,
> Kith and kin should not
> break under strain,
> Lord as you do,
> your folk will so
> and follow as you teach.
> If brother brother impeach,
>   who will give aid?   223

Good red bow warps, be it not kept a-frame,
brothers strewn wide be 'n peril to do same.

2

So hast 'ou wrong to keep thy kin afar,
whom will they copy, if not their officer?

3

Elder to younger should indulgence show
and aid his brothers in their fortune also:
good brothers in their mutual relations
should not augment their cares and exacerbations.

4

Turgid is grutch
who clutching honours
learns no manners. One such will
ruin a canton to end all in ill.

5

Old horse plays colt,
old dolt steps out of line,
eats for three men
and is an ass in wine.

6

Teach not the ape to climb,
thou fling'st not mud
at whomso lies in mire, an thou but plan
decently
small men will swarm to thee.

7

Thick cloud moults snow
that melts before the sun
yet none
would stand aside from preferment
thinking to mount more high on falling pride.

8

Deep drifted snow the sun's eye melts away,
Man and Mao * had their day,
　　　　　　My heart! their day!

X

'Neath the thick willow 'tis good to lie,
Let the Imperial foot pass by
If he gi' me a low job it would lift me too high.

2

Better stay 'neath the willow bough
than crush a toe beneath the Imperial car,
if he gave me a lift, it would take me too far.

3

A bird can circle high over cloud,
a man's mind will lift above the crowd
reaching employ on high above us all
to dwell in deeper misery when he fall.

BOOK 8. THE OLD CAPITAL

I

For an officer
in the old Capital, fox fur
(yellow) his manner without pretense;
his speech made sense
　　　　　Ergo ten thousand now
　　　　　yearn to return to Chou.

---

* Tribes.

2

In the old Capital scholars all
wore wide plaited leaf hats and small
silk caps (black), the ladies' hair
was of a neatness that appeared unaided,
        the present hair-dos
        leave my heart unpersuaded.

3

In the old Capital officers wore ear-plugs fittingly
of seu stones (common jade) and the dames seemed
as to the manner born of Yin or Ki.
None such do we see pass
        today, and my heart is
        as smothered beneath wild grass.

4

The scholars' sash ends in the older court
had a certain grace in severity,
their ladies' side hair curved like a scorpion's tail,
something to follow, tho' we never see.

5

There was no fuss about the fall
of the sash ends, there was just that much to spare
and it fell, and ladies' hair
curved, just curved and that was all
        the like of which, today, is never met;
        And I therefore
        express regret.

II

The morning 's over and I've picked less
than a handful of green *lu* grass.
My hair 's in a tangle, I'd better go wash.

2

The morning 's over and I have got
less than a skirt-full of indigo, five days to come;
sixth: he comes not.

II·8   THE OLD CAPITAL

3

When he wanted to hunt
I cased his bow,*
when he'd a-fishing go
I carded his fishing line also.

4

Then folk would stand to watch him pull out
tench or bream, bream or trout.

III

Soft rain
High grain.

Rain fats our millet sprout,
ours, who went on and out
under Earl's urging.

2

We pushed and heaved and prodded our oxen,
crowding the road, saying how home was good
to come back to.

3

Massed men about cars moved in close order
saying: this done, we'll go home from the border.

4

Close was the work at Sie under Shao's urging.
Shao's Earl planned it,
manned it, finished it all with due ardour.

5

We cleared the slope and the plain,
cleared streams and the springs, by Shao was the settlement;
the King's heart is now content.

* Graph is "long leather" meaning presumably that she took the bow off the rack where
it had been tied to keep from warping, and put it in a leather hunting sheath.

Berry leaves in marsh, thick as leaves can
be. 'tis joy to see a gentleman.

Mulberry in the low-land low
gloss of the leaf,   'tis so
much joy to see   a true man.

Mulberry covers the low-land glade with
shade that lets but small light through,
Honesty holds men together like glue.

I have held him in love so long,
from heart's midmost be it song
not to be lost.

White the marsh flower that white grass bindeth,
my love 's afar,
          I am alone.

2

White cloud and white dew shun,
amid all flowers, none.
Steep are the steps of heaven
          to him unknown.

3

The overflow seeps north from the pool,
rice hath its good therefrom;
singing I sigh
for a tall man far from home.

4

Are mulberries hacked to firewood for the stove?
A tall man, hard of head, wrecks my love.

5

Drums, gongs in the palace court
are heard by passers by,
yet if you think at all
of my pain, you think but scornfully.

6

Tall maribou stand at the dam,
cranes cry over dry forest
that a tall man teareth
the heart in my breast.

7

Drake at the weir spread a wing to the left in amity,
in man's unkindness his mind
is scattered as two against three.

8

These flat thin stones will not raise
me high enough to see
him who embitters my days.

VI

230

The silky warble runs in the yellow throat,
never kept katydid to rote
                         unceasing so —
yet comes to rest in angle of the hill.
Roads to go,
loads how?
Drink, eat,
think as taught,
carts ought
          to carry us, carry us on.

The silky warble runs in the yellow throat,
bird comes to rest by angle of the hill,
a road 's to go, needs must
that never comes to end,
drink, eat,
think as taught,
carts ought to carry us, carry us on.

The silky warble runs in the yellow throat,
birds in hillside abide,
dare we not go? Needs must
fear dust, bars end, but on,
drink, eat,
think as taught,
cars ought
          to carry us on.

The host pours, tastes, offers, and
then receives back the drinking
cup in his turn.

Take and boil but a melon leaf
so be good wine is to pour,

be but one rabbit head to grill or roast,
amid gentlemen the taste 's in the toast.

Be but one rabbit head to roast or grill
if for the toast wine there be,
taste, offer, and take back the cup. Good company
maketh all the feast savoury.

VIII

Where the torrent bed breaks our wagon wheels,
            up, up, the road,
the mountain stream runs far;
            toil, toil, toil, to the East is a war
and no leisure.

Where the torrent bed breaks our wagon wheels
            up, up, the road steep
and the mountain stream runs far;
            toil, toil, toil, to the East is a war
and we to it.

Pig wades in wave, full ford; rump 's white
            as moon in the Hyades.
That means yet heavier rain; we, levied East
            get no white ease.

IX

Lily bud floating, yellow as sorrow,
grief today, what of tomorrow?

Gone the bud, green the leaf,
better unborn that know my grief.

Scrawny ewes with swollen heads,
the fish traps catch but stars.

What man has food now
after these many wars?

X

Yellow, withered all flowers, no day without its march,
who is not alerted?
Web of agenda over the whole four coigns.

Black dead the flowers,
no man unpitiable.
Woe to the levies,
are we not human?

Rhinos and tigers might do it, drag it out
over these desolate fields, over the sun-baked waste.
Woe to the levies,
morning and evening no rest.

Fox hath his fur, he hath shelter in valley grass,
Going the Chou Road, our wagons our hearses, we pass.

PART

THREE

in three books

THE
GREATER ODES

BOOK 1. DECADE OF KING WEN

1

**The simplicity and written civilization
of Chou supersedes the bronze
and luxury of Yin-Shang.**

> Glare King Owen, rooted above,
> light as the light of heaven.
> Chou, though old, had
> the decree, twice-given.   235

Bright, aloft, Wen, glitteringly,
Chou, tho' an old regime, gat new decree;
Had not Chou been there like the sun's fountainhead
the supernal seals had never caught sun's turn
that King Wen tread
up, down, to stand
with the heavenly veils to left hand and right hand.

2

Untiring Wen that hath untiring fame,
such order and such resource by him came
to Chou with sons and grandsons of Wen,
to sons of grandsons and collateral,
root, branch, an hundred generations; and all
Chou's officers; is it not said:
Such source is as of light a fountainhead?

3

Is he not so the sun above his clan,
and they the radiant wings gleaming to flank?
Think on the lustre of our officers
born in the kingly state,
whom this state bred and holds; Chou's pace
orders them all — to King Wen's quietness.

4

Wen, like a field of grain beneath the sun
when all the white wheat moves in unison,
coherent, splendid in severity,
Sought out the norm and scope of Heaven's Decree

till myriad Shang were brought under fealty.
Shang and his line in all their opulence

5

Now stand in livery for Chou's defence, that all
may know Sky's favour is not perpetual,
so no man's luck shall hold.
Yin men, now, when we pour
wine to our manes, stand about the door
with tiger's grace and ease,
clad in their antient splendid broideries,
faithful at court and in the battle line,
mindful what NUMEN stands within the shrine.

6

Mindful what manes stand here to preside;
what insight to what action is conjoint,
long may we drink the cup of fellowship,
Yin's pride in mind, always to show the point,
a tub of water wherein to note
thy face. Had Yin not lost the full assembly's vote
He had long held to drink with the Most High,
yet mistook fate for mere facility.

7

High destiny 's not borne without its weight
(equity lives not save by constant probe)
Be not thy crash as Yin's from skies, foreseen.
The working of Heaven hath neither sound nor smell,
Be thy cut form of justice as Wen's was, shall rise
ten thousand states, thine, and with candour in all.

II
Referring to Yin-Shang as Yin to
avoid confusion with Ta-Sheng, names
having very different ideograms which
do not confuse the eye in the Chinese
text.

236

O light that shineth neath dire power aloft
(mind was below, above: blood-might to harm)
The heaven 's not solid, and to reign 's not soft.
Yin could not hold th' inherited empire neath his arm.

2

When of Yin-Shang, Jen, Chy's second daughter
wed into Chou and was brought up to court,
by lucid insight, honest in her deed, she
made in her body Wen, of King Ki's seed.

3

And this King Wen, attentive in his mind,
wide-soaring in observation,
so clear in serving the power that is on high,
designing in his heart felicity
from inwit to his act moved ever so straight
he got in sovereignty the whole Quadrate.

4

The Skies looked down and two fates came to nest,
Wen began action, Heaven raised up his mate
on the North Banks where Hia meets with the Wei,
Wen laudable in his stance and she
                    heraldric heiress of the Palatinate,

5

of that great House, who seemed
a younger sister of Heaven. Wen after smooth augury
went out to meet her at the ferry of Wei,
bridging that stream with boats and pageantry.

6

The seal was from heaven, to Wen this destiny
in Chou's high seat, and Hsin's first born his queen
who in her strength bore Wu, the augmenter of fate
who, after the "Flame of Words" * laid Yin prostrate.

7

The hosts of Yin
were as a forest in route.
For the oath at Mu spoke out: I begin this
and well. Shang-Ti is near you now,
let no man doubt.

* I take it, the Great Declaration. *Shu* V.1(3).

8

Then the plain overflowed with the flashing of hard-wood cars,
black manes and the dash of the bays,
Shang-Fu in the van always
as a crested eagle soars,
And Wu, the King, fluid cool *
layed out so towering Yin
and in the clear light of the morning
inspected his men.

III

As gourd-vines spread, man began
leaf after leaf and no plan
overgrowing the Tsü and Ts'i,
living in caves and in stone hives
ere ever they knew a house with eaves.

2

Old Duke T'an Fu galloped his horses †
along the western water courses
along their banks to the slopes of K'i
and took Lady Kiang for his company
to set up the House of Dynasty.

3

Dark violets filled the Chou plain
and thistles sweet as an artichoke ‡
where T'an 'gan plan
and to invoke
the scorched divining shell.
"Time: now; place: here; all's well,"
said the shell, "Build wall ad hoc."

4

Gave men comfort and quietness;
settled, right, left, with boundaries;
with laws, drainage and harvesting,
from West to East all was to his ordering.

* The battle order to the troops at Mu (*Shu* V.2) was to stop and reform after a maximum
of six or seven steps forward and at most four, five, six, or seven blows struck.
† 1326 B.C.
‡ "as a dumpling," what other thistle?

III·1   DECADE OF KING WEN

5

He called assistants for all this,
called a proctor of prentices
to build him a house, to build them a home;
with plummet, tightened frame boards, and line,
raised a temple to his forebears
with wings wide to the moving airs.

6

Earth in baskets for the wall, lime at call;
whacked it with paddles, scraped and beat,
scrape and repeat,
each day 5000 feet,
moving faster than the drum beat.

7

Reared they a great draw-bridge and gate
and a gate of state with a portcullis;
built also the great chthonian altar
for hecatomb ere they went to war
or did any other large business,

8

Some trash T'an could not annihilate
but held to his honour at any rate;
cleared out the bushy thorn and oak
to make road for travelling men
and so discouraged the hunting hun.

9

Then King Wen brought to civility
the lords of Yü and of Ju-i;
taught 'em to bow and stand aside,
say: after you, and: if you please,
and: this is no place for barbarities.

IV

238

Thick oak, scrub oak men pile
for fagots; order in government
hath power, to left and right, tensile
to zest men's interest.

And order is held by the split seal and mace,
His honourers are long-haired suitable officers.

Many and many oars take boats on Ghing
to meet the king of Chou's six army corps.

And as

The Milky Way sets rule aloft in sky,
in his longevity the king of Chou
has raised up men distantly.

To make true form as metal or jade he grinds;
as needle that draws on silk,
draws on the whole nation's mind.

V

239

For deep deer-copse beneath Mount Han
hazel and arrow-thorn make an even, orderly wood;
A deferent prince
seeks rents in fraternal mood.

2

The great jade cup holds yellow wine,
a fraternal prince can pour
blessing on all his line.

3

High flies the hawk a-sky,
deep dives the fish,
far, far, even thus amid distant men
shall a deferent prince have his wish.

4

The red bull stands ready, and
clear wine is poured,
may such rite augment the felicity
of this deferent lord.

5

Thick oaks and thorn give folk fuel to spare,
a brotherly prince shall energize
the powers of air.

III·1   DECADE OF KING WEN

6

And as no chink is between vine-grip and tree
thick leaf over bough to press,
so a fraternal lord seeks abundance
only in equity;
in his mode is no crookedness.*

VI

Three generations to make a gent

T'ai Jen Wen's mother, by her orderliness
won grace of Chou Kiang, dowager
of the Royal House.
T'ai Sy made triple ply, as chord to their tone
of fame; we count
her an hundred sons as if her own.

2

Kind to the manes of the ducal hall,
He nagged not against their timing,
gave no offence at all in any season;
patterned his mate,
which pattern his brothers caught;
thru whom he managed clans and the state.

3

In court suave concord,
at rites, reverence;
presence invisible,
effortless support.

as the sun draws up
the vapour's thread
tho' unseen.

4

Mid swirl of great evils not to be set aside,†
had courage to respect perfection,
a pattern till then that none
had heard tell of; and to investigate
abuses not codified.

* Last line is echo'd in the Tennin's speech in Hagoromo.
† Not till his son Wu won the victory of Mu plains.

5

Therefore focussed men even now
fit acts to inwit; youth starts,
but men of old had stamina to carry it thru;
their glory: elegance
asserted officially.*

VII

**How King Wen received the
succession, his attack on Ch'ung.
All this before the battle of Mu.**

White God above,
thine eye in awe
looked down and saw
neither Hia nor Yin
trusted of men;
probed the great states,
their walls, their hates,
and only to West
one clan stood test.
He therefore led
Chou to kingstead.

2

Raised up a screen,
cleared brush and vine,
levelled the land's lay
(terraced the slopes)
dug ditch, set hedge trees,
whip-stalk and tamarisk;
drove out the Kuan horde
(the "string tribes")
Light to lead action
heaven shifted,
Drinking with heaven
Chou had the lordship;

* The ode is full of terms that become technical in Confucian ethics. *Analects* XVI.xiv;
Chung Yung XV; *Mencius* 1.I. 7, 12. "Don't lie down on it."

III·1 DECADE OF KING WEN

3

Neath Sky's eye on hill,
cut oak and thorn tree,
lined pine and cedar,
A state he founded
And men to king it
from T'ai's time to Ki.
King Ki, kind of heart
took his brother's part and rent
so to apply it
that with glory
the Four Coigns had quiet.*

4

Sky gauged the mind of Ki,
silently fame
marked out his straightness,
which then shone out
and shining knew to choose;
advanced in technique
lordly to attend the voices,
then was king,
ruled a great state, obeyed
and knew proportions.
And so we come to Wen —
inwit and act conjoint —
anointed of the sky;
sons of his grandsons
still hold empery.

5

Out of the Welkin
came the word to Wen:
Burn not to deviate,
to kindle and grab
at every lust's desire.

First to the Mount, saw Mi in jactancy
daring so great a state,
invading Yüan, raiding as far as Kung;

---

* T'ai convinced that his nephew Wen was most fit to rule, abdicated in favour of Wen's father Ki, presumably the third brother of T'ai, not next in seniority. Thus eliminating both his own sons and senior nephews.

Blazed in his anger, mobilized, blocked out the horde;
made Chou secure and so qualified
to take the empire in his stride.

6

His base the capital;
invaders from Yüan's edge
climbed to high crag and ridge
but got no slopes
or upland pasture dales,
neither our springs to be their water supply.
Pools, springs, ours, south of Mount K'i
the pick of the plain
measured in homestead, in land made fit by the river Wei;
Wen suzerain
over the ten thousand fiefs of the plain
(and measuring square).

7

Then God to Wen: I mind me the equipoise
bright in thy act and thought,
a decor without great noise,
neither mnemonic nor as a lesson taught
but following fluid the pattern cut aloft.
Sky then to Wen, the king:
Ware of thine enemy; bring
brethren, hooks,
battering rams, all
great carrochs and go
against Ch'ung wall.

8

Great carrochs and the arbalasts creaked slow,
giving Ch'ung time to parley beneath the wall;
Questioned the prisoners, slow, one by one,
almost in silence the left ears fall,
seeking the sanction from the Father of War
that all in the four squares be rightly done,
first in the camp-site; second, before the town.
Then to the catapults! and Ch'ung is down.
High Ch'ung is down and hath no exequies,
her rites are out
and to land's end no man defies.

When he planned to begin a spirit tower
folk rushed to the work-camp and overran
all the leisure of King Wen's plan;
old and young with never a call
had it up in no time at all,

The king stood in his "Park Divine,"
deer and doe lay there so fine,
so fine so sleek; birds of the air
flashed a white wing while fishes splashed
on wing-like fin in the haunted pool.

Great drums and gongs
hung on spiked frames
sounding to perfect rule and rote
about the king's calm crescent moat,

Tone unto tone, of drum and gong.

About the king's calm crescent moat
the blind musicians beat lizard skin
as the tune weaves out and in.

IX
WU, AS THE GREAT FOOT-PRINT

King Wu in their spoor,
three wise kings were set over Chou,
Avatars now they be in heaven over all
while he drinks with them in capital.

2
Drinking King's cup in capital,
seeks their insight where right to drink must
hatch from folk's trust, he
builds for long dynasty.

3
Perfect the trust.
A map to man,
thinking what sonship could be,
he taught all sons filiality.

4

Men sought him as man to man,
his deeds done from heart-sight
taught men how right is done
when paternal nature lasts into son.

5

Lasting light is ours like a great rope
from Wu "the spoor"
unto ten thousand years, while skies endure.

6

Luck down from heaven,
homage from the four coigns in, to pack
ten thousand years. Shall he lack
acolytes?

X

WANG HOU CHENG TSAI

Praise to King Wen for his horse-breeding,
that he sought the people's tranquility
and saw it brought into focus.
                              WEN! Avatar, how!

2

Wen had the Decree and war-merit;
when he carried the attack against Ch'ung
he made Feng capital of the province.
                              Wen! avatar, how!

3

He solidified the walls of its moat;
He raised Feng on the pattern
not hasting at whim, but in conformity, filial,
                              A sovran, avatar, how!

4

The king's justice was cleansing
and the low-walls were four-square at Feng
even throughout the kingdom
the kingly house was their bulwark,
                              A sovran, avatar, how!

III·1   DECADE OF KING WEN

5

Feng water flowed east
that was Yü's spinning,
the four squares were even,
Splendid the rule over princes,

                    Emperor, avatar, how!

6

In Hao was the capital and the half-circlet of water,*
From West from East from South from North
none thought to break order
(no man but wore Wu's insignia)

                    Emperor, avatar, how!

7

He divined, to the 9th straw of ten in the casting
that Hao be the capital for his dwelling;
The tortoise confirmed it; Wu brought it to finish,

                    WU, avatar, how!

8

Feng water makes the white millet;
Did Wu not choose his officials?
He bequeathed the design to his dynasty
that their line feast and at leisure.

                    Wu, avatar, how!

* 1134 B.C.

THE CREATION
(of mankind, or of the Chou clan)

HOU TSI, John Barleycorn, settles in T'ai.

DUKE LIU, the magnanimous, in Pin
(allegedly about 1796 B.C.).

THE DUKE SHY OF SHAO addresses
King Ch'eng (possibly 1109 B.C. or thereabouts).

DUKE MU OF SHAO, in time of
disorder under King Li
(the "changed odes," IX, X) 877–841.

THE EARL OF FAN, idem.

1
"Prince Millet," J. Barleycorn, Hou Tsi

245

Mankind began when Kiang Yüan poured wine
to the West sun and circling air
and, against barrenness, trod the Sky's spoor.
Then, as a sudden fragrance funnelled in
and to its due place,
a thunder-bolt took body there to be
and dawn Hou Tsi, whom she bare on his day
and suckled presently.

2

Saith legend: was full moon, and effortless
the first birth was as a lamb's, no pain, no strain,
slit, rent, in auspice of the happy spirit in the child;
the upper sky unstill, unslaked by sacrifice?
intent on this kindling birth.

lamb,
burning
babe

3

And, by tradition, he was "Cast-away"
in narrow lane to lie
suckled between the legs of kine and ewes.
There be to attest
that he was Cast-away in flat forest

wherein the woodmen found
(hacking at trees) Hou Tsi upon the ground
and on cold ice, warmed by a bird's plumes
till the bird took flight
whereon he howled to welkin with such might of sound
it filled the wood-paths and the forest around.

the
snow
bird

4

Then crept aloft to the hill-paths of K'i
and to High Crag
whereon, to eat and mouth, planted broad beans
which gave leaf suddenly.
Rice was his servant, ripe, more ripe;
hemp and wheat stood
over the fields like tent cloths,
melons gat laughing brood.

5

Was Hou Tsi's harvest mutual process?
Howkt out thick choking grass,
put in the sound yellow grain
that squared to husk, filled out its sleeve to full
as it would burst the ears, unmoulding and tasteable
bent there with weight of head
durable; so had in T'ai his stead.

6

From him we have first-class seed, our classic grain:
blacks, doubles, reds and whites.
To keep blacks, doubles, they be stacked a-field.
Red and white yield
we bear a-back to barn
or shoulder high,
wherefore Hou made the rite yclept "return."

7

What is our rite, become traditional?
Some hull, some take from mortar, winnow or tread,
some soak (or sift with ever shifting sound)
and boil till steam and rising fumes abound.

Some turn to augury or plunge in thought
and kindle southern-wood with moon-like fat
leading the ram to cross-road sacrifice
on spit to turn, heating the seeds a-field
so to insure next year full harvest-yield.

8

From heaped plate and clay dish the odours rise
to please, in season, the power above the skies
by their far-searching smell that fits the time.
Hou Tsi began these rites. The folk of Chou
unblemished have maintained them until now.

II
FESTAL

Tough grow the rushes, oh!
No passing kine break down
their clumpy wads, and blades so glossy growin'.
Our brothers all be here at call
assembled as to rule
wherefore lay down the mat, the mat
and bring the old man his stool.

2

Put a soft straw mat on a bamboo mat
let lackeys bring in the stools,
toast against toast, wine against wine
observant of all the rules,
then rinse the cups and bring catsups *
with pickles, roast and grill,
trype and mince-meat and while drums beat
let singers show their skill.

3

The trusty bows are tough, my lads,
each arrow-point true to weight
and every shot hits plumb the spot
as our archer lines stand straight.

* Karlgren fancies a bit of tongue in the menu and someone else has a note on kidney
sausage.

III·2   DECADE OF SHENG MIN

They shoot again and four points go in
as if they were planting trees,
For a tough wood bow and the archers row
attest the gentilities.

4

An heir to his line is lord of this wine
and the wine rich on the tongue.
But by the great peck-measure, pray in your leisure
that when you're no longer young
your back retain strength to susteyne
and aid you kin and clan.
Luck to your age! and, by this presage,
joy in a long life-span.

III

"Per plura diafana"

strophe 3

247

Drunk with thy wine, but with thy candour filled,
Prince, to ten thousand years, felicity.

2

Drunk is thy wine and ready is thy food,
May'st 'ou for ten thousand years give light to thy brood,

3

With a clarity that doth as vapour rise,
Good moon enjoin such ends
as be from planting the ghost's voice commends.

4

What such commending?

"Thy dishes here be clean."
Friends lend an extra ear
to whom, in awe, maketh his justice seen.

5

Who honoureth right order, timely,
His line shall last
filial, enduring, not to be declassed.

olim de
Malatestis

6

What thing is class?

House, garden, lady's path,
let them stand for ten thousand years,
dignified aftermath.

7

What is succession, what posterity?
May heaven quilt soft thy rent
and for ten thousand years let there be
cortège and host to follow thy decree.

8

How shall be cortège?

Heirs to thy consort,
Consorts and heirs be theirs
to fill thy court.

IV
ON WEI NEAR HAO

Ducks on the river King
the dukes' ghosts come to hall
for banqueting
quiet and all
Clear wine, good food for manes set,
their mood at this banquet
that joy be more perfect yet.

2

Ducks land on sand,
Dukes' ghosts in hall,
where all is as all should be
many wines make much revelry,
and who eats as the Sire's ghost
shall know prosperity's utmost.

3

Ducks by isle,
the dukes' ghosts come to hall
to have quiet withal,

clear wine, thin sliced smoked meat,
where the ghosts of nobles eat
felicity shall be complete.

4

Ducks there where the rivers meet,
the ducal manes come to eat,
wherefore in templed hall
Felicity makes festival.

5

Ducks in the gorge, as thru the fragrant fume
the ghost is come,
Wine to taste, baked meats to nose,
where ghosts feed come no future woes.

V
THE SUN SPIDER
in the ideogram Hien

At leisure to take delight,
Tensile his virtu is
who leads his folk aright,
and their officers; his rents
from heaven, he augments,
fate that the skies renew.

2

A thousand rents, an hundred luck's intake;
his grandsons multiply.
White wheat a-field and glory upon high,
fit prince, fit king
errs not, forgets not, but leads men by
antient legality.

3

Respect for equity keeps well defined the crown,
fame of clear conscience fructifies the deed.
No grudge, no hate,
leading as though on parity
with the multitude, luck comes unboundedly.
He makes, to the four coigns, all orderly.

4

Holding the end threads
over his dinner table in amity.
Appointed ministers, princes of birth
all watch his eyebrows, and the work goes on,
the official work.
Of common men everyone
has his own earth.

250

VI

Duke Liu, the frank,
unhoused, unhapped,
from bound to bourne
put all barned corn in sacks
and ration bags
for glorious use, stretched bow
showed shield, lance, dagger-axe
and squared to the open road.

2

Duke Liu, the frank
looked to the plain afar
to help his many and multitude,
conforming (to geography)
he issued an order accordingly.
They grumbled a bit and then clomb high
to the ridge and echo of Yen Mount and then
came down to the plain beneath.
His only boat was of green jaspar
that gleamed at the tip of his sword-sheath.

3

Frank Duke Liu
passed by the Hundred Founts,
saw the wide watershed,
clomb to the South Mount's head;
scanned site for capital
to o'erhang the wild:
a time to dwell in house, a time is meant
to live in bivouac, a time to tell
tales and make argument.

4

Duke Liu, the frank,
based on his capital
spread order thru
that land as on swift foot,
gave mat and stool
to whom should mount or lean in cenacle.
Sent to the cattle-fold,
pork was from sty
and wine from calabash
for all the templed line
to drink and eat.

5

Duke Liu, the frank,
measured the hills to know the light and shade,
dark female and light male, the wide and long,
where land would answer, where to prod in seed;
how the springs drained, and to three army corps
measured the marsh and plain
all to be channelled fields for tithe and grain,
measured the South West slope,
so dwelt in Pin
where desert waste had been.

6

So lodged, in Pin, Duke Liu
fixed fords on Wei,
whetstone and anvil rock (for stepping stones).
Gave them based house and laws,
assembly and land-tenure
even to Huang Vale and the torrents of Kuo
both banks, to river bend,
many were housed and all was made secure.

VII

Cleared by its flowing, dip the flood water up
and it will steam thy rice or other
grain; a deferent prince is
to his people both father and mother.

Rain-water cleared by its overflood
if thou ladle it out will wash thy altar jar;
To a fraternal prince will his folk
return, as to home from afar.

In a fraternal prince his folk have rest,
as from rain water
cleared by its flowing thou hast
a pure house, or thy garden is blest.

VIII

Around the hill-bend the south wind whirling,
Prince, in your brotherliness
coming at ease to sing
unhurried, let these notes fit your turn.

2

Say is friendship leisure's test,
best of leisure giveth rest,
Prince, for your young-brotherliness
in such life as rest confers
may you live and drink wine with your ancestors
and so your life reach term.

3

May you to earth and sky at crux of winter,
Prince in all deference
reply, and set firm the calendar
when, turning beneath his cliff, the sun goes hence.
May an hundred spirits of the air allied
gather to banquet where you preside
and so your life reach term.

4

You have received it: dynasty
for how long? To enjoy great rent?
Prince deferent,
the candour of a House is its longevity.

5

(Rashness is, fortitude is)
There are the filial,
there are those who see straight
to take action to lead;
to shelter. Young and fraternal prince, be thy pattern
such that the four coigns heed.

6

O source and height,
jade sceptre, bright fountainhead,
Think what your fame can be
and what men hope, Prince brotherly, that hold
the square of the realm on guiding rope.

7

Hark to the phoenix wings astir in the air,
Here is their bourne, here is their place of rest,
Old and tried officers crowd round the throne
to know thy will, now thou art Heaven's son.

8

Old and tried officers crowd round the throne,
Hark to the phoenix-wings at heaven's gate,
Let him appoint such as will keep touch
with the folk of his state.

9

Hark to the phoenix' song
o'er the high ridge amid dryandra boughs
that face the rising sun,
thick, thick the leaves,
so calm serene that song.

CODA

The Lord's wagons be many,
his fast horses trained better than any,
And a few verses will make a song
when there's a tune to drag it along.*

* I see no reason not to take this as a coronation ode in three parts. St/ 1–3; 4–6; 7–10. Or 7–9 and 10 as coda. Circa 1109 or 1116 B.C. No one will deny the presence of ambiguous passages in the original. The chapter in the *Shu* (V.12) is of particular interest in bearing directly on the tradition.

IX
Duke Mu to his colleagues in the ministry,
avoiding lèse majesté in the form.
First of the "changed odes,"
in King Li's time. 877–841 B.C.

253

Folk worn out, workin' so late,
Kind rule at centre hauls on a state.
Pitch out the slimers and scare off worse,
Thieves and thugs see a light and curse;
Easy on far men, do with what's near,
And the king can sit quiet the rest of the year.

2

Folk worn out need support,
Men gather round a kindly court;
Throw out the punks who falsify your news,
scare off the block-heads, thugs, thieves and screws.
Don't shove it off on the working man,
But keep on doing what you can
                    for the king's support.

3

Folk worked out need time for breath,
Kindness in capital
draws on the four coigns withal;
Sweep out the fakes and scare the obsequious
thugs, thieves and screws
and don't promote the snots to sin on sly.
Respect men who respect the right
and your own honesty may heave into sight.

4

Folk burnt out need a vacation,
Kind court alleviates people's vexation;
Throw out the flattering fakes,
scare blighters and crushers,
Don't ruin folk pretending it's government,
tho' you're mere babes in this business
and the job bigger than you can guess.

5

Folk burnt out need a little peace,
Kindness in middle causes no injuries.
Turn out the oily tongues and parasites,
thieves, squeezing governors; don't upset honest men.
The king wants jewels and females,
I therefore lift up these wails.

X

Attributed to the Earl of Fan
in King Li's time, 877–841 B.C.

254

The sky's course runs a-foul and in reverse,
a jaundiced people sink beneath the curse.
Given to untruth plotting never a-right,
You say, and lie, that no sage sees the light.
                    Against your nearsightedness
                    I employ this reproving verse.

2

The heavens send down the hard, pull in your smirk
Gainst sky's square kick, no man has time to shirk.
Words fit to fact
folk will enact;
Calm discourse
needeth no force.

3

From a different line of work, my colleagues,
I bring you an idea. You smirk.
It's in the line of duty. Wipe off that smile, and
as our grandfathers used to say:
Ask the fellows who cut the hay.

4

There is no joke in heaven's severity,
Old men clear ditches and young men step high.
My word 's not moss-grown. Your frivolity
is a muck heap's blaze.
Fagots, not to be saved, blaze higher,
Medicine grass puts out no fire.

5

Dour heaven 's not cogged to fit your jactancy,
Good men sit corpse-like still, perversity
is your line. The people groan,
none dares ask why
all 's wrack, no charity.

6

Light's lattice, the sky aloft, tunes man
as flute or pitch pipe can;
easy to lift as half
the jade tally-mace, none tries to enlarge his half to tune.
Prone to untune, be not yourselves the base
of their untunedness.

7

True men a fence, and serried ranks a wall,
Great states a buffer, clans as a flank bulwark.
Straightness in action gives calm. That meditate,
Clan-chiefs shall be as solid thy stronghold,
let it not moulder here till solitude
be not thy worst to fear.

8

Revere the anger of heaven
nor count it vain stage-play;
Revere the motion of heaven, bawl not thy jactancy,
The light of heaven is clear enough to see
the king going out, and at sunrise there's light
enough to show
the revel's remnant, idleness' overflow.

BOOK 3. DECADE OF T'ANG

I

255

Wide, wide aloft, Sky's overhanging power,
Fearing the curse, divers the fates and many.
Man's multitude
is of heaven, all born, and none
can trust to fate alone.
They be few who conclude.

2

King Wen said: So!
Towering on high
Yin-Shang, taxers run wode beneath your tyranny,
oppressors unbounded beneath your tyranny
by you hold office and in uniform
Heaven made them evil, but you hoist their power.

3

King Wen said: So!
Yin-Shang insatiate,
one honest appointment arouses hate,
The over-steppers of boundaries answer
with a flux of debate.
You set thieves in the core of your state,
Then wait in wishful thinking
and make no move to investigate.

4

King Wen said: So!
You brawl in the middle kingdom;
collect resentments and call it sincerity.
There is no light in your conscience
and your acts shed, therefore, no light
in your inwit and you are left without ministers,

         without party.

5

King Wen said: So!
Yin-Shang not tanned of wind but of wine
red. Not in virtue's line
moving, wrong in your stance,
You have taken a tiger's roaring for pattern
and think that mere noise is a form.
Having neither light nor darkness to norm,
neither darkness nor light,
You bed at dawn and rise up with the coming of night.

6

King Wen said: Huh,
Yin-Shang aloft there,
Your noise is like bugs in the grass,   cicada,
as the bubbling of soup in a cauldron.   broad
              locust

Great and small are near to destruction,
your arrogance sprouts by the roadside,
You enter the middle kingdom to tyrannize
and the pest spreads to the Devil's dominion.

7

King Wen said: So,
Woe to proud Yin up aloft,
It is not that skies are unseason'd,
Yin useth not the old wisdom.
Even tho' there are no old men and perfect,
the antient statutes remain and he does not hear them,
                    The great seal is broken, cast down.

8

King Wen said: So!
Damned Yin, there is a saying:
              Utter destruction is knowable
Tho' branch and leaf be unwithered
           the root is rotted away.

Yin's reflecting tub was not far distant,
It was in the generations of the dynasty of the Hia.*

II

**Ascribed to Duke Wu of Wei,
who reigned 811–756 B.C.
He reproves himself, at the age
of 95. Vide also Ode 220.**

**Control, control, in awe of ownership
That angle be clear twixt what is mine and thine.**   256
                **Anal. corner XVII.16;
                Mencius I.i.V.1.**

Show of respect is held as virtu's sign,
Thus the old saw was meant:
No man 's all-wise, plain
men are fools as of their natural bent,
the sage's nonsense runs against the grain.

* Presumed to be by Duke Mu, in the time of King Li's disorders, 877–841 B.C., recalling
great precedent.

2

First seek out manhood,
four coigns will follow this, give thee assent
in word; study thine inwit to shape thy business,
four realms will agree in mind 'thout argument.
Lofty ambition is reached by calm decree
so be the far scope is proclaimed seasonably.
Revere all straightness, respecting thine and mine,
thy pattern shall the whole folk's form define.

3

How stand we now? Confusion in government,
bemusèd chaos up, and conscience down,
flat down, be it on back or front,
but sunk at any rate — thou art so drunk
and deep in nothing save it be merriment.
Severed continuance, thou dunce,
shallow in law of antient kingly light
that might, in this darkness, tow thy bark aright.

> With false diffuseness
> in seeking precedent,
> losing the clear
> and penal laws intent.

4

Disorder hath no preferment from the sky;
as the spring's seepage that runs wallowing down
with no clear channels, it but sinks, is lost.
Wake with the sun and go thou late to bed,
dust out thy court-yard and sprinkle, folk will take
order. Attend to thy carts and nags,
bows, arrows and weapons, for the land's defence
'gainst the wild Mann and crude South's insolence.

5

Weigh your appointees to their natural weight,
measure your feudal lords attentively
lest ructions come upon you unaware.
Mean from the heart what flows out from the tongue;
respect your own respect for equity
nor lack true tenderness.
Flaw in jade sceptre can be ground away,
'gainst word ill-spoke there is no remedy.

6

Glib not with facile speech,
no man can gate thy tongue vicarious.
Words cannot die and pass,
every fool speech begets its argument,
unright begets reply in unright's zone.
Be just in recompense, stand by thy friends,
be father to all folk of little means
and your wee'uns' wee'uns shall be
a line grown to a rope: posterity,
none without heritor.

7

Meet not thy friends with scowls,
Error 's yclept almost vicinity,
and when thou art thine own sole company
say not: No man can see thru the roof's air-hole,
In my north-west ingle is naught can make shame,
here is no eye.
The spirits have their own divisions of thought
not to our measure wrought,
that ours yet shoot toward.

8

Prince, 'tis thy job to keep thy conscience clean
inducing so a probity
laudable.
Care for the place you're in, plant there your tree,
defect not toward men's rights in property
either by theft or gentler usurpation
and you'll be followed, almost, by the nation;
Peach thrown to me, shall net a plum for thee
and . . . lambs will have horns, my son,
when rainbows turn to stone.

9

Tough wood will bend
if silk 's to make the string,
Calmness curves men and conscience is their base.
Wise, at these words, mere words, old saws,
do right, while fools deny,

run to reverse, and call them my tyranny
to prove: *quot homines, tot sententiae*
                    (each man, his mind).

10 [*still himself to himself*]

I took thy paw ere thou knew'st fair from base;
Showed thee the how, which when thou wouldst not face,
grabbed at thine ear. Dost thou plead ignorance?
And a father of grown-up brats? We fear . . .
We fear that men are incomplete,
Cock-sure at cock-crow and naught done by night.

11

Bright is the light that gleams in over-sky
yet leaves me grumped in black stupidity,
grinding it out, over and over again,
the self-same lesson, which, if thou dost hear,
art bored contemptuous, not bored to tears.
Dost 'ou plead ignorance?
                    After these ninety years?

12

This is the spot, the old stand is not changed,
but can'st 'ou act? can'st do it? That 's the rub,
to keep the people from yet greater woe,
tho' heaven frowns pestilence and state 's to wrack?
Take parallel, thou hast not far to go
nor doth sky err.
Defilement of inner light
brings blight,
and dire, on all thy folk.

III
**Ascribed to the Earl of Jui,
who died 827 B.C.**   257

Soft shade of these mulberries
was a fit place for ten days' ease
but they keep hackin' away,
people's itch is no comfort to me,
heart levelled up with misery

I look to the burnished sky
that might look down again pityingly.

2

Here be four hefty nags
with a flutter and flap of falcon flags
and an unendable hullabaloo,
every state government fallen thru,
nobody left wearing black hair,
jinx on the remnants everywhere,
howling and mourning and every grief
and the kingdom rotten to its last leaf.

3

Also the state's money has given out,
given out and flowed away
and heaven has nothing to say;
under suspicion, nowhere to stand.
Jump off? nowhere to land.
Gentlemen could of course combine to run the state
without acrimony and party line.
Well, who started it anyhow?
And who the devil can stop it now?

4

I brood on the land's woe and house woe
born out of date
to early grief,
from west to east no relief,
no quiet, and as for thorns round the gate!

5

Think, damn it, on the brink
of ruin, I tell you to think,
and appoint solid officers, wet hand
for hot iron (you can drown
in a stream while discussing the best way to filter it)
even hot iron will sink.

6

North wind blows breath down the throat,
the people are decent, you head 'em off;
love hay-ricks because they are power
over the people, not because they are food stuff.

You treat grain
as if it were jewels and porcelain,
it is hoarded in silos instead of being used
for food in good will.

                    7

Death rains and chaos from heaven down
swamping the king and throne,
worms gnaw thru root and joint of the grain,
woe to the Middle Land, murrain and mould.
Prospect of plenty is sudden emptiness,
no strength for the troops in this distress
to think of over-arched nothingness.

                    8

A kind prince hath men's respect
for his mind's grip, plans' scopes,
and for the care he sets to select
right men to aid him.
But this cantankerous top
thinks he alone is right
and guided by his own sole liver and lights
ascribes the trouble to the folk's uppishness,
grown uppish (and from him) over night.

                    9

Observe in the middle wood pair'd herds of deer
in contrast to false friends among us here.
Slander grows no good grain
and, as the old saw says:
Roads both ways
run thru valleys
(such is their natural route).

                    10

A wise man's words
are heard an hundred *li*,
A fool delights
in his own jactancy.
Sans words, no power,
Why fear, why jealousy?

11

The good man is not wanted, is not pushed on,
The tough guy 's on the make from dawn to dawn,
with folk always a-letch for stress and storm
although rank poison would be better for 'em.

12

Great winds move clear
thru the great hollow vales,
Good men avail likewise
as if thought's form made the grain rise.
Dirty dog must
perforce find dust.

13

Great wind to tomb,
Greed, so, is doom.
Could he hear and reply
to what I mutter drunkenly
for his good,
utterly misunderstood?

14

And will you, friends, say that I sing
in ignorance, that I know nothing, yet sing?
Beasties on wing
time's dart shall touch presently.
I was your goodly shade,
and your rage turns against me.

15

There is no limit to what some people will do,
Cool officials' shifty backs
do not make-good popular lacks.
They say they can't help what goes on,
alleging that people are twisty naturally
they seek force to enforce their authority.

16

The "people" are not in the least perverse
the high-ups rob, cheat 'em and do worse,

then tell you they haven't sufficient power,
polite while you're there, jip you next hour,
and then say calmly: It wasn't me.

I have therefore compiled
this balladry.

IV

DROUGHT

The Milky Dragon twists bright across heaven
and the King says: What wrong has been done in this time?
(that the rain comes not neither is promised)
but sorrow, confusion, famine,
again, yet again, neither do the spirits of air sustain us
though I have prayed to them all, grudging no victim.
The sceptre and pierced jade lie here lifeless *
                    Aude me, Domine
                    Assuage, O assuage!

2

The great drought is come as parching,
quilted with locusts and swollen,
there is no sacrifice I have not offered
neither have I neglected the bournes nor their altars,
Above, below, I have offered up offering
and I have buried.
There is no power I have not honoured,
The Lord Tsi does not uphold us
Nor the power of heaven approach us,
Waste, devast the earth,
would that it fell upon me, on my person only!

3

For the great drought I offer no self-exculpation,
I quake as under the thunder,
that there be no whole man left in Chou,
God over heaven, neither that I survive.
Why will none join me in reverence
that the spirit of the ancestral cartouche,
            the founder, the cult, come not to end?

* Or simply that he has buried all he has, to propitiate the powers of earth.

4

The great drought! None can withstay it,
It is impetuous fire against which I have no recourse.
The great destiny draws to an end,
we find neither awe nor shelter,
nor do the pastoral lords of aforetime
                              bring us their aid,
O source of my founders, carnal and uterine,
                    How can you bear this in quiet?

5

Great the drought, the high hills are parched
and their rivers withered away,
without and within the fire-demons consume us,
My heart is made barren with the sorrow of burning,
The pastoral dukes of aforetime will not hear us
neither will the bright god over heaven
permit me to lay down my charge.

6

The drought has parched into the depth,
I struggle, I labour and dare not retire.
Why comes this affliction upon us, mad with the heat,
We know not the reason.
We prayed early that there be harvest,
we have neglected no bourne of the Square,
O light that is high over welkin
this is not what we expected,
By my reverence for the bright spirits of air
they ought not to hate me.
I have had awe for the intelligence of the spirits
for the light in the air circumvolvent
they should not hold me under their anger.

7

The drought has parched deep into the earth,
the people are dispersed leaving no records,
the local governments are fallen to pieces,
the prime minister, the head of the horse-guards,
the head of the commissariat have broken down,
The great officers have done their utmost, no one has funked,
I look up to heaven, saying:
                        Where is the bourne?

8

I look up with awe to heaven,
the stars are like broom-straws and holes;
the great officers and the princes
shine as idly, giving no profit.
The great decree comes near to its term.
Do not cast off your precisions,
why seek in me the causes of local government troubles,
I look up with awe to heaven. How should it grant me rest?

V

SUNG, IN HONAN,
highest of the Five Peaks *

High, pine-covered peak full of echos,
Proud ridge-pole of Heaven, roof-tree
whence descended the whirl of spirits
begetters of Fu and Shen,
Out of the echoing height, whirling spirits of air descended.
To sires of Chou were given in vassalage, bulwarks,
under the bright wings of the sun
a square kingdom against invasion,
Strong as the chamber of winds.

2

The King set task to Lord Shen
      who is as a full altar
to carry on in his service; to set city at Sie;
to be pattern to all the South States.
To the Earl of Shao he commanded saying:
Make smooth the way of Lord Shen
that he set house in the South Land
there to form the South state
and that coming ages maintain this labour.

3

And the King said to Lord Shen:
Be thou pattern to all the lands of the South,
make use of these men of Sie;
lift a pivot that shall not shake.

* To celebrate King Süan's appointment of the Marquis of Shen to defend the South
Border, Ode by Yin Ki-fu. Süan's time 826–781 B.C.

And to Earl Shao: Mark out the lands of Lord Shen
into fields.
And to the Master of Stewards:
settle men in these homesteads.

4

To Lord Shen the labour, and to Earl Shao
the building construction
to begin the town wall and the inner temple
(to roof perfectly temple and fane)
And when this labour was ended
he gave to Lord Shen four horses,
high steppers with gleaming harness and breast-hooks,

5

and a car of state with the horses, saying:
Our plan is your shelter,
there is no land like the South
I give you this sceptre whereon to raise up your treasure,
Go forth, Uncle Royal,
and maintain the lands of the South.

6

At Mei was the feast valediction
and the Lord Shen turned south
to form true homestead in Sie
And to Earl Shao he commanded
that he lay out Lord Shen's land divisions
and set provision stations in mountain passes
that there be no undue delay.

7

So the Lord Shen came to Sie
in due order with cohorts
with footmen and charioteers
and through all Chou was united rejoicing
for such solid defence and good bulwark.
Was not the Lord Shen as a sun drawing vapours,
the Royal Uncle, ensample in peace as in war?

8

And the Lord Shen acted on conscience
by mildness and probity bending the thousand states,
Be he famed to the four coigns of all things.
Ki-fu has made this song
the tune and the text of it
to be as a wind of healing
As his gift to the Lord Earl of Shen.

VI

Heaven of fire and water
making man
had stuff and plan;
put there matter and sheaf
took grip in seed
to natural good disposed.

260

Water above, fire beneath
so man had, from heaven, his breath,
                        a vapour,
matter and form compact,
seed and cord held intact
                        to love
natural heart
            shown in act.
Sky saw the holder of Chou
clearly attent
on humble folk's betterment,
so made and sent
Chung Shan-fu
to maintain this Child of Nature
                        in Chou.

2

Chung Shan was pattern of praise
handsome of face as of ways,
with a mind for the antient laws
ever detailed. In vigour of equity,
By his concord with the Sky's Child
an enlightened destiny prevailed.
            (And Chou's rule spread).

3

This was the King's command:
Chung Shan set hand
to form the hundred princes, and —
as from Chung's Source it was, and heritage —
to guard the king's body, promulgate, report;
be the king's tongue and throat;
levy, and govern outer borders and palatine,
that the four coigns keep line.

4

System in Royal decree,
in Chung Shan, aptitude
to know the states, good and not good,
astute to use his light,
to keep himself himself, uninterruptedly *
day, night,
serving the Monarchy.

5

"Eat soft, spit hard out," so the proverb says,
In Chung Shan's case, the rule was put in doubt.
Poor widows and fatherless were not insulted
Nor to encroaching bojars indulgence granted.

6

Men have a saying: 'Ware,
virtue is light as a hair,
few can lift it, most gaze
(contemplatively) at honour's ways.
Chung lifted it, and wd/ rely
on no man's affectionate partiality,
where failed straight letter of the King's decrees
Chung Shan-fu filled in the deficiencies
      (patched up the royal robe).

7

Cross-road sacrifice when
Chung Shan set out,
strong his teams.

* *Ta Hio*, K'ung 4.

Light of foot, in his battalions,
every man eager to pace the stallions,
"pang, pang" and
rein bells chink when Chung Shan-fu began
the great East wall
at the King's command.

8

Four fleet stallions on rein the
eight rein bells jangled away
when Chung Shan-fu went out to Ts'i,
Here 's a hope for his quick return,
Ki Fu lifts this neat bordone
with clear sound as wind over wheat
That Chung Shan's mind from labour long
may come to quiet at least in a song.

VII

On Balk-hill high Yü began
terracing fields. That road, his way, still manifest,
so the Lord Han had his charge from the king direct:
"Ancestral right, but waste it not,
ever alert, by day, by night,
not easy to fence lands of the sort
whose lords come not to court,
thereby giving Us support."

2

With four great stallions tense
on rein, the Marquis of Han went to audience,
By royal grace held tally-mace, flag, palio;
got chequered car-screen and embossed brass yoke,
black robe, red shoes, and for his team,
breast hooks and frontlets engraved,
a leathered front-board with tiger-fell
and metal rein-rings as well.

3

At the cross-roads Han sacrificed,
nighted at T'u. Hien gave him the parting feast,

clear wine in an hundred jars, and large menu:
roast turtle and rare fish with garnishings,
sweet sprouts of young bamboo,
and, as a parting gift, team, chariot
and paraphernalia plates, as fits clan feast.

4

Kuei-fu's daughter, King Fen's niece,
Han had by hand such royal piece
to meet at Kuei's with an hundred teams,
bells a-din, catching the light.
The escort girls about her were like clouds
unto the Marquis' eye,
and the great wall-gate flamed with
that splendour of pageantry.

5

Kuei-fu by war, then, had passed thru
all states, none missed, and, when he sought
site for his daughter's homestead, knew
none to match Han in pleasauntness.
Rivers tend great greenness to send there,
fish in abundance be mid this fertility,
bream, tench. Doe and deer cry mating where
roams many a bear and great bear,
lynxes and tigers there be. His child Han Ki
could have, thus, home there delightfully.

6

Wide be the walls of Han,
Yen troops had capped them tight.
Font of this dynasty got charge
in causal time, mid hundred tribelets, to be lord,
Marquis of Han, over the Chui and Mo horde
and great lands North, to be
their Earl because of solid wall and moat,
ploughed lot and register
and pay tribute in pelts
of the white fox, red pard and yellow bear.

VIII

How Hugh Tiger of Shao went
against the South Tribes,
over the Kiang (825 B.C.)

Kiang and Han
                    crashing along,
A river of men
                    flowing as strong,
Never a stop,
                    never astray,
When we went out a-hunting
                    the wild tribes of the Huai,
Out with our cars
falcon-flags clack,
never a halt,
no broken rank,
when we marched to outflank
                    the wild tribes of the Huai.

                    2

Turgid the waters of Kiang and Han,
a glitter of men
                    flow rank upon rank.
As threads on a loom
                    done as to plan,
We sent dispatches up to the throne:
"The four coigns are quiet,
in four coigns no riot,
Let the King's commons live quiet."
There was, so, for a time no unsettlement
and the King's mind was content.

                    3

By green Kiang banks,
By green Han banks
The King ordered Shao Tiger
to make model state administration:
open it all four square
for cultivation,
tithe and define,

III·3   DECADE OF T'ANG

with no sudden demands, no extortion,
but as Royal Domain to perfection utmost
set there bounds, forms and laws
even to the south sea-coast.

4

And the King commanded Hugh Shao:
Ten days, wide proclamation:
Wen and Wu received the Decree, and the Duke of Shao
was their bulwark.
Count me as a child, be thou like him,
go into function; judge;
make use of your fortune (the grant)
the light come to rest upon you.

5

"Measured to you that you should measure in turn
by sceptre-spoon, wine from the holy urn,
clear jade to lift out the black-millet's breath
that Wen above (spirits above) may know in Earth beneath
hills, lands and fields are set in your account
as from the ancestral fount in just accrue
take up this charge from Chou (in Chou)."
And as the grain bows, Hugh bowed then:
"Ten thousand years, Sky's son, to be thy span."

6

Low as the grain falls, with his head to ground
bowed Hugh: "Royal grace manifest,
let it so rise that the Great Duke may attest
it unto ten thousand years, Sky's Son,
in the brightness of his mentality
may the fame of his mind know no end;
as an arrow may his civilized insight penetrate
by act the four realms of the state.

IX

THE CONTINUING VALOR

Concerning King Süan's expedition
against the Huai further North,
ode attributed to Earl Shao,
Duke Mu, hero of the preceding.
The aim being comfort of
the border states of the Sü.

263

SPLENDOUR ON SPLENDOUR, LIGHT OF THE MIND TO ENLIGHTEN:
The King to his Minister,
Huang-fu of the line of Nan Chung *
High Commander:
That he set in order the six army corps;
That My weapons be sharpened;
That there be awe and a warning
as a kindness
to the States of the South (to defend them).

2

The King said to the Head of the Yin clan:
Order Hiu-fu Earl of Ch'eng to make flank defence
left bank and right bank,
to alert (police) all my regiments
that march by the reaches of Huai,
that he keep eye (care for) the lands of the Sü
that there be no dawdling and no billeting
and in the Three Services most exact coöperation
to the one end.

3

Splendid, dire, terrible in magnificence
the Imperial operation royally
stretched out, supported, aroused
with no gaps and no straggling,
ever deploying and prodding.
Sü land was shaken by the hooves of the cavalry
as sky under wings of thunder.

4

The King lifted his war might as a bird from a field nest,
as anger of thunder;

* For Nan Chung, vide Ode 168.

he sent out his tiger-dragoons
growling and roaring like tigers
they moved out ever more thickly by the sluices of Huai.

With captives ever more under paw
the Huai banks were sectioned
and King's arms there to hold them.

5

Many and thick moved the king's troops
as the wings of birds flying
(as the red plumes of the pheasant);
as flood of the Kiang and Han,
as the gnarled roots of the mountains,
as rivers o'erflowing
undulant as bright wheat, and continuous.
None could measure them, none could stay them
and they cleaned up Sü-land.

6

The king's candour was clear and continuous,
Sü land came into the kingdom
therein to have equal equities
by the work of Heaven's anointed,
Sü land was quiet,
The Sü came to the court-yard:
"In Sü there would be no twisting."
Whereon the King said they could go home.

X

Ascribed to the Earl of Fan,
against King Yu, 780–770 B.C.   264

I look up with awe to the exigeant heaven
which hath no kindness to me-ward,
my unquiet is come to the full.
The sky presses down heavy as whetstone
nothing moves calm in this country
officers and folk are afflicted
boll-weevils in root and joint
gnaw, spread pestilence
and there is no end to this evil,
criminals are not apprehended,
there is no easy reform.

2

The Royal Domain has over-run private holdings;
if the feudal lords had retainers, you have usurped them;
the people are as birds in a net,
the innocent lie in the sprung trap of the stocks,
and the criminals walk up and down boasting.

3

Wise man rears a wall
and a sly bitch downs it,
so nice to look at, elaborate in contriving?
No. Dirty, an owl, her tongue long as a dust-storm.
The stair-way, confusion not descended from heaven
but up-sprung from women and eunuchs
from whom never good warning nor lesson.

4

They attack willful to injure, in this wise:
Their first slander passes unnoticed,
there is no bourne to their tattle,
as if a nobleman did not know the nature of usury
at three hundred per cent ("in the manner of trade")!
Keep the hens out of public business,
let 'em stick to silk-worms and weaving.

5

Why is the welkin thorny
that the powers of air do not bless us?
you even shelter the wild tribes of the North
and turn hate against me,
you do not look to the signs of the times,
you disregard justice,
men resign from their offices
and the uprooted state is worn out.

6

Heaven is come down like a net
all-taking, and men go dolorous into exile,
heaven is come down like a net
hardly-visible,
and men go into exile heart-broken.

7

High spouts the water, from the hornèd spring;
deep grief.
Neither before nor after but come now
that sky should work as mole beneath the grass
and nothing is
beyond its power to thong.
Wrong not the light that brought thy line to be
and might save, still, sons coming after thee.

XI

Attributed to the Earl of Fan 265

Compassionate heaven, O thou autumnal sky
hasty to awe, famine is here, now surely death draws nigh,
Folk die and flow to exile in the waste,
dead homes and stables are hidden beneath wild grass.

2

Heaven has let down a drag-net of ill-doing,
the locusts have gnawed us with word-work,
they have hollowed our speech,
Perverse alliances and continuing crookedness have divided us,
evil men are set above us, in ease.

3

Amid slanders and vain disputations
they see themselves flawless,
they know not their errors
they count on their not being seen,
emulous, ostentatious, cantankerous in their ostentation
by long disorder
the high offices are brought down.

4

As grass in a drought year
with nothing to water its shoots,
as cress in dry tree fork, dry as a bird's nest
so in this state
there is none not given to sabotage.

5

Former prosperity stood not on a chance of weather,
nor does calamity now.
They have dredged up their rice,
why don't they retire from office,
and the older ones first?

6

Pool dry without inflow,
Fountain dry without inner spring,
they have overflowed wide with their injuring,
they have engrossed and expanded their functions,
may they not overwhelm me.

7

When the king (Süan) got the Decree here before you
he had a Duke of Shao to uphold him
who brought the state an hundred *li* in one day;
Today they lose daily similar holding,
and as to the nature of sorrow
there are men who do not strive to grasp the antique.

PART

FOUR

in three books

ODES OF THE
TEMPLE AND ALTAR

I

Wholesome and clean the temple space
with health and clarity of the grain;
ordered the harmony and pace
that gentlemen sustain assembled,
gathering what King Wen's virtue sowed,
that is frankness of heart,
straight act that needs no goad.

He who is gone beyond is now the norm in sky,
the map and movement whereto these conform;
as is above, below,
not manifest, incarnate from our sires in span;
needs not dart forth, but is here present in man.

II

Tensile is heaven's decree
in light and grain without end.
As the pure silk (that tears not)
was the insight of Wen,
and he acted upon it.
In its beauty are we made clear,
its beauty is our purification
                 as we bow at the altar.
Be strong his line to the fourth generation,
may his great-grandsons be strong.

III

Clear, coherent and splendid,
King Wen's dissociations,
continuing use hath perfected,
they are bound in the felicitous program of Chou.

Fluid in clarity,
from mouth to ear binding, scintillant;
scrupulous, enkindling,
King Wen's classifications initially
tracing the lines of our worship,
the spirit moves in their use;
hath brought them to focus.
Chou maintained their enlightenment.

IV

Ardent in refinement Lords-dividers, Lords-justices,
source of felicity, chthonian, and of abundant
kindness to us without bourne;
great-grandsons sustain this.

No tally-mace but to your state,
kings and clans think of merit and prowess
continuing solid this empery
effortless, binding humanity
that the four coigns obey.

Most manifest the insight that goes into action
in forming the whole state service,
thus the kings of old pass not into oblivion.

ALITER

The unviolent (or unwrangling) man
shall the four coigns obey,
whose lucid thought is in act, not in display.
On his instruction many princes form,
nor shall oblivion wreck this norm.

V

Sky raised this hill, high hill
T'ai Wang found waste, dressed (ruled).
Wen had his rest,
beat its rocked trails to roads, K'i's roads
that his sons' sons maintain.*

* K'i means a hill trail. The K'i are the dalesmen, alpini.

Dawn, dark, he laid the covert, close-packed foundation
in coherence, in splendour
twisted the cord of brightness;
by his mind's oneness he
built calm into Dynasty.

271

Light above heaven focussed the decree
doubly on dynasty (in Wen and Wu) then came

King Ch'eng, who daring never to rest
early or late, bulked in the bases,
close-knit, intimate,
coherent, splendid in ardour,
by his heart's singleness
spread order to the land's utmost recess.

VII
Hymn for princes at audience in the
Hall of Light, end of Autumn, sacrifice
to God and King Wen.

272

We bring, we give
a ram and bull alive,
Let heav'n stand right.
King Wen's law is our light;
Sun clears four coigns,
that is Wen's joy.
He's accepted.

Day, night, in fear
of heaven's majesty,
our bread shall he be.

VIII
As spoken by the Duke of Chou
on tour of inspection after
Wu's overthrow of Shang,
and thence afterward at
commemorations (?)
"The legality of his kingship binds in
the continuity of the sovereignty."

273

In season to ride the bounds:
Light over sky through sky
this son is its leaf.

Solid and dexter order holdeth Chou
at his light word to shake
and none shake not,
three fields (T'ien, Hao and Wei)
spirits awake; comply
as in his breast
so in hill crest
the powers of air attest
concord
to Huang Ho utterward;
Light to the mind from Chou
forming to all men that shall sit on thrones.

King in legality
continues his sov'reignty
"Lay down your weapons now
put by shield, lance and bow,
arrows also.

"I seek to nourish all,
as my mind sees
        may my deed fall."

"Hia outseasoning
I swear to uphold the king."

(? considered as the
King's words)

(? oath in response, both
by the Duke, or later
commemorators, and the
chief assistants?)

274

IX

Great	hand	King	Wu
vied	not,	made	heat.
He	drew	not as	sun
rest	from	work	done.
Shang-	Ti	(over	sky)
king'd	our	Ch'eng and	K'ang;
bound	all	four	coigns;
hacked	clear	their	light.
Gong,	drum,	sound	out,
stone,	flute,	clear in	tone
ring	in	strong	grain;
bring	here	hard	ears.
Work,	true,	shall	pay.
As we've	drunk	we are	full,
Luck	ev-er	is and	shall
Come	with	new	grain.

IV·1·i   THE TEMPLE ODES OF CHOU

Think to thine art, Lord Grain.
By thy power to drink down
cup for cup of heaven's own
stablish thou us by damp and heat.
Without thee is naught complete,
barley and wheat from thee we cull,
Over-sky gave thee the rule
how to feed us. Lead us,
not by this field bourne held in,
that the fruitage ever run
in seasons of the Hia's sun.

THE TEMPLE ODES OF CHOU
ii. Ch'en Kung

I

Wards of the fields   respect the laws of grain
see that the tithe be just (as king, so laws)

Come test, come eat.

Aids of the wards   now is the end of spring,
what more's to seek
tho' field be old or new?

White's on the wheat,   come now 'tis clear as day
bright is the sky above
at last 's to use the strong and quiet year.

Fate of our multitude, so tell them fate:
who readies his spud and hoe
shall not reap late. They mow beneath your eye
and light's aloft, packed tight
wheat grains are in ear.

Imperial wheat
receive their intelligence.

Augur, oh King Complete, by thy light's point,
gleam of the ray that falls from thee, at ease,
(We from the altar call)
lead on thy peasants all;
show sowing day.

Swift then and up in every family field,
grant that each thirty *li* of this tilled land yield
ten thousand rationings.
We plow by twos.

Egrets to fly
to this West Moat,
guests at my portal
be such cause for joy.

No hate roots there,
and here in court no irk,
but as the seeds of motion are
to all their folk, early and late
cause praise.*

Full be the year, abundant be the grain,
high be the heaps composed in granaries,
robust the wine for ceremonial feast
and lack to no man be he highest or least,
neither be fault in any rite here shown
so plenteous nature shall inward virtue crown.

Blind making sound,
much sound
in the temple court,
Chou's court,
carved frames
and tiger-stands,
high teeth
and rangèd plumes

* *Ta Hio* IX.3.

Drum sound shall make the "field,"
stone gong, the "stall,"
with bamboo's ordered tones to "left" it all.
Lordly voice, played,
over-played
processional of sound
reaching the shades
as their audition is
in this sound's mysteries.

Sound, blind sound,
teach our ancestral shades
where guests outside the gate
insatiate remain
desiring perfect sound
last,

Guest facing ghost
to time's utmost.

VI
CONSERVATION HYMN,
for the first month of winter

281

> ... θεῷ ἱερὸν ἰχθύν,
> ὃν λεῦκον καλέουσιν, ὃ γάρ θ' ἱερτατος ἄλλων.

Lo, how our love of god is shown in fish,
here be all sorts in sacrificial dish
such as our grandsires' sires offered of old,
we have conserved them, manifold
blessings, held from age to age
by men who shun all forms of sacrilege.*

VII
282

Quiet as waters flowing in a moat
before great tripods princes move about.
The Son of Welkin stands as a field of grain.

---

* Icthyological dictionaries available to Karlgren give two kinds of sturgeon. Legge
ventures further: thryssa, mud-fish and yellow-jaws.

Here is the great bull brought for sacrifice,
assistant manes round the altar rise,
O great white Source, O thou great sire of all
see how thy sons and theirs are filial.

The constant voice shall all thy temple fill
for peace, for war, our conduct thy delight
as former Kings and latter wrought aright.

Bushy the brows of venerable age,
grant they be ours, O far, great spirit assuage!
Father and maker, that the spirits come
To prove they be not sundered in the tomb.

VIII

They come for talley-rods,
bright dragon-flags display'd
glittering, jangling
rein-bells, and dash boards.
Here be the princes
led to the fane,
Bright shone the ancestral eye,
filial this majesty.

Thick be the brows of age
so long sustain'd,
mind ye the imperial luck:
ardour, and skill, princes and dukes,
strands twined to felicity,
given coherence, given zeal
pure wealth and common weal be one
clear light on agèd altar stone.

IX

Welcome to the representative
of the former dynasty, Shang;
this is shown by the dynastic
colour of the horses

A guest, a guest and a white stallion,
his escort a battalion
honest to stand there as cut in stone,
guest for a night and a night, and twice,
right (whom we can trust, trust.)

Give him a tether to tether his team.
Left, right, courtiers gleam,
easy to say: reflect, recall,
go with him further on his course, meditate:
all quiet throughout the state —

that on his line, once loud in majesty
the heavens pour down untimed felicity.

X

Wu royal,
if we inherit
age-old quiet
'tis by his merit.

285

Not by envy in his zeal
Wu king'd the Imperial rule;

Wen by his learning won
what has been from that time on.

Wu had the heritage;
layed low Yin-Shang's rage by arms
and left to us our world of quiet farms.

THE TEMPLE ODES OF CHOU
iii. Tho' I be lytl (Min yü siao tsy)

I

KING CH'ENG

286

Tho' I be lytl, alas, come soon to care,
sick with its weight I hie
to the ancestral majesty
duty that lasts with lasting line for aye.

Tho' I be lytl, reverent I am
from dawn till night
of the high king's light,
the threads that he as our first preface wrought
shall not pass out of our thought
if so that thought
stand by the altar stone
where first it shone.*

* 1116 B.C. *Shu* V.xiii; V.vii.

I seek a bourne and stop mid river grass,
led by the gleam that my dead father lit;
follow the time's divisions that he set
and find no magic herb no *molu* yet.

I am not deep to rule such family cares,
move thou, my father's spryte,
up, down this court: bulk of my aid,
so be my body in bail to assure thy light.

III
CH'ENG, THE YOUNG KING,
on the monarch's duty to observe
the seasons and calendar

Awe is upon me,
thought from heaven pours down,
No light fate his who comes young to the crown,

Nor may I say that heaven is there, remote,
high there, unreached, aloft above my head
to mount and sink, star after star's scrutiny
enters our destiny.

I, but a child, must choose whereon to stand,
by sun, by moon, counting the sky's command;
study to know how men of old caught stars
and by their light
saw time to act, cleaving the wrong from right.

IV

Whenas my heart is filled with kings and deeds
seeking avoid the cause of new regret,
take not a wasp for bird that has no sting.
To see what moves, and snatch, solves nothing yet.
Wall built sans plan is wall soon over-set,
neither can rest who would always show wing.

Gainst high scrub oak and rathe to plow the marsh
pair'd plowmen went, attacking gnarl and root;
pacing low slough and ordered boundry dyke
what crowd is here: the master and his son,
aids, wives and food; strong ready neighbour men
sharpened the plows, so came south fields a-grain.

A power from far and silent in the shoot
see how the spirit moves within the corn
strong as a stallion, quiet as water on tongue.
Here be the stalks a-row, silky and white;
wave as a cloth beneath the common sun.

Ordered the grain and rich beyond account,
fit to distil to drink in sacrifice.
Let manes come to taste what we devise
agnate and cognate. As pepper to ease old age
here without altar shall be holiness
not now for new, but as it was of old
tho' tongue be light against the power of grass.

Speed, speed the plow
on south slopes now
grain is to sow
              lively within.

Here come your kin,
baskets round
baskets square,
millet 's there.

With a crowd of rain-hats
and clicking hoes
out goes the weed
to mulch and rot
on dry and wet,
crop will be thicker on that spot.

Harvest high,
reapers come by
so they mow

to heap it like a wall
comb-tooth'd and tall

an hundred barns to fill
till wives and childer fear no ill.

At harvest home kill a yellow bull,
by his curved horn is luck in full
(be he black-nosed seven foot high,
so tall 's felicity.)

Thus did
men of old
who left us this land
to have and to hold.

VII

**Probably for the day after
sacrifice to the representatives
of the ancestors**

292

Let robes be of bright silk,
caps reverent worn.
From hall to gate-house base,
from ram to bull,
from great tripod to small

bear the great rhino-horn of holy curve.
Sweet the wine,
be gentler still thy mind. If now
thy thought be sage
it shall sustain thee in thine old age.

VIII

δικαιοσύνη

To conclude a dance in honour of Wu

293

A delight of metal was the king's host,

he obeyed the seasons,
he provisioned when the sun lay dark in the matrix.

In the day of purity and of ardour
he used the Great Intervention
when the sun lay plumb on the dial.

We dragoons receive (favoured) what the high king built,
may we use his dissociations.

Be justice the basis of faith
in this army.

IX

**Sung in connection with a dance
to Wu, and, in declarations of war,
to the war god. Said to date
from the time of King K'ang.**

294

Tranquil'd * ten thousand states,
year after year of abundance,
that the heavenly ukase change not,
the horn was not cut off.

O dawn in the forest,
steady sun amid boughs,
Wu,
King,
guaranteed there should be such officers,
the four coigns to have quiet.

Calm was
in his house
that its light gleamed up to heaven,
filling the space between. He was Emperor
as if at his ease.†

X

**Said to contain the formula
used by Wu in granting fiefs
in the Dynastic Temple**

**When the season was full
to the sun's turn
the silk was unravelled.**

295

King Wen worked where he was
(established position)

We properly answer; receive.

* *Shu* V.vii.
† *Analects* VIII.xvii (VIII.xxi).

IV·1·iiiTHE TEMPLE ODES OF CHOU

Spread with the sun's turn
due order of thought into the uttermost.

We go out to seek the quiet procedure,

the time of Chou is of destiny
to the utmost order of thought.

XI
"THE P'AN," that is, the "transport song,"
which I take to mean the one used
when carrying the talley-jades
to Wu and to his successors
in his capital

296

In bright season
Chou was risen;
mounting High Mount,
passing Proud Mount
crag to echo on peak of Mount Yo.

Wings of water in Ho
packed thick, ever to flow
over all spread
neath Heaven's lid.

Gather the talleys at turn of the sun.
Time, Chou, and fate are one.*

BOOK 2. THE HORSE ODES OF LU
εὔιππος

I
KIUNG KIUNG MU MA

297

Wild at grass the bull horses
move over moor-land,
black-rump'd and roans,
all-blacks and bays,
a splendour for wagons, unwinded.
Phang! Phang! I'll say some horses!!

* *Shu* V.xiii, 24; "in response to the people."

2

Strong, sleek, move wide over moor-land, bull horses
dapple, piebald and bay,
strong on the traces
mixed white hair and yellow,
there is no end to his thinking of horse power.

3

At graze over moor-land strong stallions
whites and bays with black manes
and white-maned black stallions
pull with due order, unwinded;
Our lord's thought is unflagging
for the breeding of horses.

4

Wide over moor-land at grass the bull horses
iron-grey, sleek, calico, dapple
fish-eyed great stallions for cars,
So our lord's thoughts bite
and his cavalry charges.

II

YU PI

Strong sleek   roan teams
That seek   the duke
To light his government,
day, night,
so do the egrets wheel ere they alight.
Drum beat and dance
maintain delight with wine.

2

Sleek stallions   and strong
early and late   to court
bring men, drums, wine. Men
come, go, come yet again
as egrets on the wing
and take their firm delight.

3

Strong sleek   gray teams
that seek   the duke,
stand near the banquet hall.
Be this inaugural: vintage to plenteous years
and to the prince sound grain
that his line maintain
for sons unto sons in ever firm delight.

III
P'AN SHUI

Joy by the sickle-pool, cress there to gather,
Lord Lu approaches, his flags together, the dragon banners
wave as the cress-leaves; horse bells clear sounding,
none seeking precedence, pell-mell yet orderly
all for long riding.

2

As thought delights in water
by the half-circling pool
picking pond-weed,
hooves clicking clearly
high feet of horses:
clear his fame, clear his face,
clear his laugh is, to teach without anger
in this place.

3

mallows beside the pool are light to gather,
Lord Lu approaches for wine and feasting.
Heavy the wine to lighten age,
by the long pilgrimage
wild tribes were bent to the sage.

4

As a white field of grain, Lord Lu
acting by light
of his insight
respecting straightness
in awe of the equities, the people's canon and rule,

loyal in peace, in war
before the fane brilliant to carry on,
a filial son,
what the Lord of the Cartouche began,
seeking in himself felicity,
antient lucidity.

5

Clear was the mind of Lu, his insight
guided his acts aright;
raised then this college by the crescent pool.
The wild Huai came neath his rule.
Tiger dragoons bring trophies here;
captive by pool-brink risketh an ear;
as by Kao-Yao the questioning,
brought to the water's encircling.

6

Officers to assembly defined
spread Lu's type of mind,
inwit to act; so, when they attacked,
swept out to East and South
by zeal and clarity o'erthrowing barbary,
neither with shouting nor with splurging
nor with recourse to military tribunals
as faithful retrievers brought their deeds to this pool.

7

The long, horned bows
volley compact,
in the cars' manège war-skill appears
uniting unwinded
infantry and charioteers, overswept Huai.
Till here
be now tillers who were vagrant rebels aforetime,
as solidly planned, the Huai are now faithful dependents.

8

Wild flapping owls flock'd to the crescent's trees
eating their fill of the grove's mulberries,
have now our tone proper at heart.
The Huai, that is, learnt civilities, in art

and in exchange bring rarities,
tusk and tooth ivories
and tortoise shells
with southern metal for crucibles.

IV
LORD GRAIN

The secret temple is still and consecrate,
solid the inner eaves.
From limpid thought to act
Kiang Yüan moved straight
till the awesome sky
filled her with its progeny.
Nor ill, nor hurt, nor distant moon's delay
hindered, so she brought forth Hou Tsi.

The hundred boons descend by Tsi:
millet and grain by him do multiply,
thick grain and panicled, the early and late
(early for bread, the late for sacrifice).

By pulse and wheat
Tsi got a state
tho' small, he taught the people all
to sow and reap
the early grain and the late, the rice, the black
the whole earth through;
followed the work of Yü.

2

Of Hou Tsi's line came T'ai,
king on south slopes of K'i,
first to trim jactancy
of overweening Shang.
Then Wen and Wu concluded that King T'ai began,
neath heaven's governance and hour
by Wu's ado:
"Have no split aim, nor doubt"
in Mu
plain polished off Shang:
"God's eye, and Shang's at end."

In this work all had part *
and the King said: Shu Fu, unkle,
your eldest son
shall be Marquis of Lu
and your great opening house shall be
wheel-aid to Chou.

3

Thus was the Marquis made lord of the East,
to him the hills and streams in lasting fief.
Now Duke Chuang's son
of Chou duke's line
comes with the dragon-flags to sacrifice,
holding the six tough reins.

Spring, Autumn, there is no break
nor ever error in this sacrifice
to the holy sky, its power
and to Hou Tsi, first ancestor.
Red bulls are slain, unsplotched, approved
by the high powers, moved
to light and plenty, and is
Chou's spirit here adjoint
to Sky and T'si.

4

For the Autumnal rite,
in summer, bulls, one white
two red, wear boards across their horns
to keep them whole.
The great libation jars
are prepared and one 's shaped like a bull.
Boil'd and roast pig, minced meat and soup
are set on stand in great and little trays.
A thousand dancers in maze
assert the heir prosperous.
Thus, eager, in fane, wave after wave
of the dance portrays:

long life and steadfastness,
stay of the Eastern State
That Lu be regulate

* _Chung Yung_ XXVI.7.

'thout fail or fall
'thout shake or quake
three antient friends shall stand
solid as crags and balks
to uphold thy hand.

5

So the Duke has a thousand cars,
Red the tassel, green the bow-band,
heavy the bows, two lances stand
upright in every car,
thirty thousand of infantry,
casques with red strings of cowries' shells
in regiments compact, act;
breast the wild tribes, the dogs,
north, west, King, Shu, and war
none dares before
Chou's arms.

6

Honour and glory and long years to fleck
hair faded yellow, the plump round back
and old cronies for argument,
who still know what that glory meant,
to be old with you in governance
endless years as a thousand pass
and in those years
under old brows, no injuries.

High holy T'ai-Shan mounts o'er craggy Lu,
"Turtle-" and "Cover-heights" we passed through
overgrowing the waste Great East
till we came to the salt sea coast,
There the wild Huai were evened out,
nowhere the allegiance left in doubt.
Lord Lu worked it so.

7

Upholder of Yi and Fu, both,
overlord of the House where had fallen Sü
and so came to the salt sea coast
Huai and the wild men of Man and Mo
and yet further the southern hordes
acknowledged these overlords, Lu.

8

Heaven assigned him such unmixed rule,
and in his age, that he uphold Lu state
to live in Shang and Hü, resume Chou Duke's domain,
Lord Lu
that he feasts in joy
with mother grown old and spouse,
his proper great lords and officer corps
of states and lands to have and bequeath
that many and all have felicity
with old men's hair and children's teeth.

9

Pines of Tsu-lai,
Cypress of Sin
were trimmed to measure and brought in,
cut to eight feet by one foot square,
with their pine beam-horns and carven heads
lofty in chamber and corridor.
The new sun temple intricate
Hi Sy raised it, high and great,
ten thousand may it accommodate.

BOOK 3. THE ODES OF SHANG
This being the oldest part of the Anthology

I

NA

301

Thick, all in mass
bring drums, bring drums
bring leather drums and play
to T'ang, to T'ang
source of us all, in fane
again, again, pray, pray:
Tang's heir, a prayer
that puts a point to thought.

With thud of the deep drum,
flutes clear, doubling over all,
concord evens it all, built on
the stone's tone under it all.
T'ang's might is terrible
with a sound as clear and sane
as wind over grain.

Steady drum going on,
great dance elaborate,
here be guests of state
to us all one delight.

From of old is this rite
former time's initiate,
calm the flow
early and late
from sun and moon concentrate
in the heart of every man
since this rite began.

Attend, attend, bale-fire and harvest home,
T'ang's heir at the turn of the moon.

                        II
                KYRIE   ELEISON
                    father of all our line
                    KYRIE   ELEISON!   302

Vintage in autumn, light of old,
iterate and no end,
be this in every man, and be thou here.

We have brought clear wine,
reward our exact thought;
our broth's to taste,
cut herbs in proper blend,
set on the stand in silence utterly,*
set in the dish and no word spoke the while:
peace in our time,

let our brows age with the years
nor be our death when they be wrinkled with time.

* *Chung Yung* XXIII.4.

Muffled the axles, studded the yokes,
eight bells with little strokes
sound the approaching sacrifice.
We had our fate of sky, ready to wide.

Calm came from sky,
abundance by aiding grain,
year after year full grain.

Come to the fane and feast
that plenty ever descend, attend,
Bale fire and harvest home,
T'ang's heir at the turn of the moon.

III
BLACK SWALLOW

303

At heaven's command
came the black swallow down
and Shang was born;
came the black swallow down
that Shang should wear the crown
in Yin, mid bearded grain, Yin plenteous.

Of old Sky told war's T'ang
to build up walls (measure the land) four square
that was the "square decree" and
thru the Nine Parts utterly
all things were squared.

Shang, the first dynasty,
never in jeopardy
stood here to Wu Ting's heir,
in Wu Ting's heirs, war's kings
having no overlords.

Ten dragon banners ride
to our high altar side
for great grain rite, father to son.

The king's domain is of a thousand *li*
that is the people's rest
and their fixed point,

all lands are measured thence
to the four seas' defence,
whence come to fane
to serve the surrounding airs
in Capitol, by Ho the bounding stream, true officers.

Yin had the high decree
rightly, as things should be
The hundred rents pour in
rightly to Yin.

IV

Out of the deep Shang's wisdom was,
long urged of stars.
Yü alone stood
gainst the great flood, and spread
it wide by the long watershed;
bounded great outer states.
Sung waits, meanwhile, its moon
till heaven chose girl to bear
Shang for an heir.

2

Dark king of the ready hand
had state with little land,
made that great, and, in the greater state
trod down on no man's right;
followed the light with deeds.
Siang-T'u in those days
swept back the wild sea's Malays.

3

The Sky's decree inviolate
stood until T'ang all orderly.
T'ang, not a day too late
came, sage, full of awe to trace
footsteps of the measuring sun
till to the very altar stone
came light deliberate.
As sky respects this order processional
so be it model, in fate,
to the earth's nine parts in all.

4

Received a small state's talley and then the great
split jade of office. Lesser fiefs
hung there like tassels on his falcon flag.
Neither contending
nor with covetousness
neither too hard
nor lax in softness,
spread his rule, tranquilly
an hundred rents flowed to his treasury.

5

Had tribute jade in lesser and great assess,
stud stallion of lesser states, a favouring dragon cloud
spread round his power
not by the thunder shock
nor heaving abrupt
but with calm confidence in his mind's use
augmented an hundred-fold his revenues.

6

The warrior king set flag upon his car,
had pity, gripped his axe and blazed to war.
None dared
stand our shock.
Three sucking shoots clamped round the King of Hia,
a stump (a block, dead wood)
None moved, none understood
(had news) in Hia.
So all the nine great holds were ours utterly,
Wei, Ku, cut down; K'un's Wu and Hia's Kie.

7

Once with time's leaf half grown
came quake and shake
whereon the heavens sent down
A-Heng * to aid the Imperial Crown,
Shang's bulwark and defence to be
solid at all points dexterously.

* Yi-Yin. *Shu* IV.4, 5, 6.

Of Yin-Wu the swift scourge,
How he fell upon King-Ch'u;
passed thru the gorges and blocked them;
bottled the King hordes and trimmed them,
thread of Shang's line, a successor,
                    OYEZ!

"O ye of King-Ch'u
that dwell in the south parts of my kingdom,
whom T'ang of old set in true order
so that even unto Ti-Kiang (the far tribes)
none dared not come to the cauldron of sacrifice
nor avoid the king's judgement:
Say now that Shang endures."

Heaven has ordained many princes,
with capitals as Yü span (and defined)
the year's works be brought to the fold
"Forfend calamity,
we have sowed and stored without interruption."

Sky ordered decent and inspection:
Attend to the folk below
without usurpations, without extravagance,
nor venture to loll back in leisure.
He commanded the lower states,
and the feudal states by seal, there was happiness.

Shang's capital high in the air and quiet,
ridge-pole to the four coigns,
Splendour of fame to Shang,
clear, washed clear in his sensitivity to prognostic
as of wings and of water;
his old age was contentment
that he sustain our kind of posterity.

They went up the King mountain,
straight trunks of pine and cypress
they cut and brought here,

hewed pillars and rafters
carved pine beam-horns ornate
contrived pillars and sockets
to the inner shrine, perfect
that his ray come to point in this quiet.

思
無
邪